# In My Father's House

Corrie ten Boom

with Carole C. Carson

**Guideposts**®

CARMEL, NEW YORK 10512

www.guidepostsbooks.com

*Library of Congress Cataloging-in-Publication Data*
Ten Boom, Corrie.
    In my father's house : the years before "The hiding place" / Corrie ten
Boom with Carole C. Carlson.
        p.    cm.—(Corrie ten Boom library)
    Originally published: Old Tappan, N.J.: F.H. Revell Co., c1976.
    ISBN 0-8007-1771-6 (cloth)
    1. Ten Boom, Corrie. 2. Christian biography—Netherlands. I.
Carlson, Carole C. II. Title. III. Series.
BR1725.T35 A34  2000
269'.2'092—dc21                                              99-045038

Unless otherwise indicated, Scripture quotations are from the NEW AMERICAN STANDARD BIBLE ®. Copyright © The Lockman Foundation 1960, 1962, 1963, 1968, 1971, 1972, 1973. Used by permission.

Scripture quotations identified PHILLIPS are from LETTERS TO YOUNG CHURCHES by J. B. Phillips. © Macmillan Publishing Co., 1947, 1957.

Scripture quotations identified KJV are from the King James Version of the Bible.

For current information about all releases from Baker Book House, visit our Web site: www.bakerbooks.com

Interior design by Holly Johnson
Front cover design by Cathy Kovacs/Enterprise Four
Back cover design by Dennis Arnold
Typeset by Composition Technologies, Inc.

When my parents were married, many years ago, they claimed Psalm 32:8 as their "life verse," the promise that they felt was God's assurance for them: "I will instruct thee and teach thee in the way which thou shalt go: I will guide thee with mine eye" (KJV).

. . . this promise became the special directive for my life as well.

*Corrie ten Boom*
*From* Tramp for the Lord

# Contents

# Foreword

Today I know that memories are the key not to the past, but to the future. I know that the experiences of our lives, when we let God use them, become the mysterious and perfect preparation for the work He will give us to do.

Corrie wrote that in *The Hiding Place*, without realizing that it had provided the introduction to this book.

As I worked with Corrie, following her around America and living with her in Holland, I saw her in many different circumstances. It is a constant amazement to me how the Lord uses her. One time my husband, Ward, and I prayed with her in a small room off a large auditorium. She was ashen with pain and weariness. When she walked on the stage before four thousand people, her voice was firm and her message animated. She was—and continues to be—a living example of the way in which the Spirit of the Lord works through His available servant.

However, as *In My Father's House* began to grow, I became excited to see how this was more than a collection of memories—more than nostalgia from a rich life. Here we had the unique lessons of a family preparing for a future, a future that would demand the power of God's love and strength.

If we are living in the time in which we believe God's plan for planet Earth is reaching its completion—when the new beginning Jesus promised will take place—then each individual and family needs the pattern for living in this present age. Never before in human history have guidelines been more important.

The applications of various parts of Corrie's life to modern living were impressed upon me as I savored those wonderful "years before." I've learned so much for my own life and family as I've lived with Corrie *In My Father's House*. Let's visit together . . .

*Carole C. Carlson*

# 1

*Inheritance*

Remarkable, extraordinary . . . Peter, where did Cook find strawberries in the midst of winter?"

The Dutch merchant summoned his butler and pointed to the luscious fruit in the silver compote. Even in the home of great wealth this was an amazing luxury in the early 1800s.

"It's the gardener, sir . . . ten Boom. He does some miraculous things in that hothouse of his."

"Ten Boom, you say. Hmm, must remember him. Astounding! Bring me some more, Peter, with lots of thick cream."

My great-grandfather ten Boom grew those plump strawberries during the chilling months when ruddy-cheeked children skated over the canals. He was no ordinary gardener, but a master craftsman who caressed the soil into performing miracles. He experimented with plants, manipulating them between an ice cellar and a hothouse, until he produced the fruit that was served at the dinner table of his employer, one of the richest men in Hofstede, Bronstede, Heemstede.

Those simple strawberries saved my great-grandfather from jail!

It was during the time of Napoleon; Europe was trembling from the onslaught of the evil little man from Corsica. Swaggering across the continent, victorious in war, the French emperor conquered country after country and forced men into submission. The government of Holland was ruled by Napoleon's followers and their oppressive regime.

My great-grandfather was an independent man; he had spunk, but not much tact, I'm afraid. He refused to submit to men who denied freedom to other men. However, Hollanders at that time had two alternatives: They were either obedient to those who served the strutting dictator, or they faced what could be very severe punishment.

Tyranny at any time in man's history demands loyalty.

One Sunday Great-grandfather went to his church and heard the minister announce the opening hymn; the theme was from Psalm 21, but as the congregation began to understand the words, one voice after another stopped. They realized it was a pointed description of their political situation. Nobody dared to continue.

But Great-grandfather and the minister sang louder, a defiant duet (translated from the Dutch):

> The evil one considers himself to be free from all
> bondage, and runs around, while he stirs the people.
> At the same time, the bad people assume they hold
> the reins of government, and they are being raised to
> the summits of honor.

Sad hearts and silent voices were encouraged by the bravery of the minister and the spunky gardener.

When news of ten Boom's traitorous act of defiance reached the authorities, he received a summons to appear at the town hall. He must have been prepared for the consequences, as he addressed the officer in charge. "What does this Mr. Snotneus [snot-nose] want with me?"

First he challenged the regime; then he hurled that contemptuous name at his accuser!

But where do strawberries fit into all this? Before Great-grandfather had a chance to be sentenced or taken to prison, his boss, who was a very influential citizen, interceded and had him pardoned. (A gardener couldn't grow fruit in jail, could he?)

My father told us this story of Great-grandfather and his personal challenge to the Napoleonic regime with a sense of joy.

"I'm glad he was a real man," Father said.

Over a hundred years later when people said to Father, "Stop having Jews in your house—you will be sent to prison," my father answered, "I am too old for prison life, but if that should happen, then it would be, for me, an honor to give my life for God's ancient people, the Jews."

## From Generation to Generation

Willem ten Boom, my grandfather, was not strong like his father, so he chose a work that was not physically difficult. In the year 1837, Grandfather purchased a little house in Haarlem for four hundred guilders and set up shop as a watchmaker.

It was in 1844 that Grandfather had a visit from his

minister, Dominee Witteveen, who had a special request. "Willem, you know the Scriptures tell us to pray for the peace of Jerusalem and the blessing of the Jews."

"Ah, yes, Dominee, I have always loved God's ancient people—they gave us our Bible and our Savior."

Beginning with this conversation, a prayer fellowship was started, with Grandfather and his friends praying for the Jewish people. This was an unusual idea among Christians at that time. The Jews were scattered throughout the world, without a country or a national identity; Jerusalem was a city torn by centuries of conflict. The attention of the world was not upon the Middle East, and yet a small group of Dutch believers met in a little Haarlem house, a watchmaker's shop (later called the Beje), to read the Scriptures and pray for the Jews.

In a divine way that is beyond our human understanding, God answered those prayers. It was in the same house, exactly one hundred years later, that Grandfather's son, my father, and four of his grandchildren and one great-grandson were arrested for helping save the lives of Jews during the German occupation of Holland.

Another strutting dictator, more arrogant and insane than Napoleon, had planned to exterminate every Jew in the world. When Holland was controlled by Hitler's troops, many Jews were killed.

For helping and hiding the Jews, my father, my brother's son, and my sister all died in prison. My brother survived his imprisonment but died soon afterward. Only Nollie, my older sister, and I came out alive.

So many times we wonder why God has certain things happen to us. We try to understand the circumstances of our lives, and we are left wondering. But God's foolishness is so much wiser than our wisdom.

From generation to generation, from small beginnings and little lessons, He has a purpose for those who know and trust Him.

God has no problems—just plans!

## Beginning with Mama

My mother was a woman with a loving sense of humor and a striking appearance. She had thick, dark, curly hair and brilliant blue eyes—an unusual combination for a Hollander. She came from a large family and was left fatherless just after her mother gave birth to an eighth baby. While she was still very young, her mother and her brothers and sisters were forced to earn their own living.

One of her sisters, Jans, started a kindergarten where Cor (my mother) and another sister, Anna, became her assistants. I'm sure this experience helped my mother later in training her own children.

When Jans added a Sunday school to her kindergarten, she began to work with a young theology student, Hendrik Wildeboer, who became her special boyfriend. Cor caught the eye of a handsome teacher in the Sunday school by the name of Casper ten Boom, and they immediately found something in common: Their birthdays were on the same day, May 18.

Romance grew between Cor and Casper; when Cor journeyed to Harderwijk to visit her grandmother, Casper was so lonely that he followed her the next day.

About fifty years later, I visited the quaint village of Harderwijk on the Zuider Zee with Father. As we walked along the Bruggestraat, Father said, "This is where I proposed to your mother. There were cobblestones instead of pavement at that time, but many of the old houses and the sea gate are still the same."

He paused to remember the youth that had vanished, and his love for the gentle woman with the laughing eyes.

"Did Mother say yes immediately?" I asked.

"No, not until the next day, and I spent a very restless night waiting for that decision!"

When I asked him if he had ever regretted his decision to marry Mama, his voice was firm. "Never! Until the last day of her life, I was just as much in love with your mother as I was on that day in Harderwijk. We didn't have an easy life—we had many sorrows—but God led us by His extraordinary providence."

## A Little Jewelry Store

Grandmother died shortly before Casper and Cor were married. By then, Father had started a jewelry store in a small house in the heart of the Jewish section of Amsterdam.

Once a customer arrived who was a pastor from Ladysmith, South Africa. He came into the shop and asked Father to provide a clock and a bell for his church tower. This was a tremendous encouragement to a young merchant. The order was simple to fill; all Father had to do was to go to the factory in Brabant to make the selection; the manufacturer did all the installation. However, the commission from that sale provided enough money for the young Dutch couple to be married.

Uncle Hendrik, Jans's husband, was a minister in a little village near Amsterdam. Mother and Father had to go to the town hall first, to be registered and married in a civil ceremony. The man at the town hall who married them thought they were "high people" because they came from Amsterdam. He tried to be very dignified, in a manner suitable for this distinguished couple, and began the marriage speech with great airs.

"Honored bride and bridegroom . . . you are now . . . you are now gathered . . . you are now gathered here. . . ." He stopped, looked around, and burst into tears.

Father said, "I'm so touched by your speech and tears, but we would like to be married."

The poor fellow finished the ceremony somehow, but Uncle Hendrik conducted the final marriage rites in his church—without tears.

The newlyweds moved into a shabby little house in Amsterdam after their wedding. It's probably just as well that the emotional clerk from the town hall didn't know of their humble means!

Mother had dreamed of a home with a small garden, for she loved flowers and the beauty of color.

"I love to see much of the sky," she often said.

The sky was there, if she stretched far enough to see it in the narrow street outside the old house. Their cramped home had a single room on each story, with worn-out furniture left by my grandmother.

Money was scarce, but happiness was abundant.

The neighborhood of Jewish people made it possible for Father to participate in their Sabbaths and other holy days. He studied the Old Testament, their Talmud, with them and was given opportunities to understand and explain the fulfillment of the prophecies of the Old Testament in the New Testament.

My father's love for the Jewish people was nurtured in the Jewish quarter of Amsterdam during those first years of married life. Father and Mother lived on poverty's edge, and yet their contentment was not dependent upon their surroundings. Their relationship with each other and with the Lord gave them strength.

## Plan for Parenthood

When the first baby was expected, Mother was glad she had learned to sew. She had inherited an old sewing machine from her mother, and every moment she could find she stitched little garments for the baby. A Jewess who lived upstairs couldn't contain her curiosity and asked Mother if she was a seamstress.

"No," Mother answered proudly, "but I'm expecting my first baby. See the little dress I've made?" She held up a dainty garment tenderly.

The Jewess was astonished. "You're not sewing the clothes before the baby arrives! That is tempting God!"

Mother was puzzled, but this didn't stop her from preparing for her baby. However, she began to understand why Mary had only swaddling clothes for the baby Jesus. It wasn't lack of money but the Jewish custom not to sew the layette before the birth of the child. I've heard that Portuguese Jews maintain this tradition today.

When Betsie, the first child, was born, Mother became quite ill. She asked her youngest sister, Anna, to come for a few weeks to help with the new baby. Those few weeks stretched into forty years.

Mother and Anna had always been close, but when Mother married, Anna went to live with Jans and Uncle Hendrik. Anna, however, became very lonely for Cor and was delighted when Mother and Father invited her to stay with them in Amsterdam.

Within seven years, four more babies were born, but

one didn't live. Father had to look for a cheaper house to accommodate his growing responsibilities.

By the time I was born, they were living on the Korte Prinsegracht, in a house at the end of the canal, where few people passed the shop. Business was at its lowest ebb.

I was a premature baby, with blue skin and pinched features. When Uncle Hendrik saw me he shook his head sadly. "I hope the Lord will quickly take this poor little creature to His home in heaven," he said.

Fortunately, my parents didn't feel the same as Uncle Hendrik. They surrounded me with love and good care. There were no incubators in those days, and one of the greatest problems was keeping me warm. I cried so pitifully from the cold that Tante Anna rolled me in her apron and tied me against her body; then I became warm and quiet.

Many years later while I was in Africa, I met a missionary family whose baby could not be comforted, until a native girl bound the child to her back with a piece of cloth. The baby became calm, secure in the closeness to the body of a person who loved him.

I must have felt that same way bound snugly in Tante Anna's apron.

Throughout the first year of my life I was a poor, sickly looking creature. Mother told me that once she was traveling by train with a friend who held a beautiful, plump baby on her lap. The baby's name was Rika, and the people in the coach were giving her many admiring glances and comments. They would look at me in my mother's arms and then turn away, unable to find anything positive to say.

Mother told me this bothered her at first, but then

she would hug me and whisper, "I wouldn't exchange you for anyone in the whole world, you darling ugly baby with the beautiful eyes."

When Rika was two years old, she began having epileptic seizures. I played with her all through my childhood, but I remember how aware I was that her little face would change so drastically as the sickness would overpower her. Mother was always ready to care for Rika; throughout her life Mother taught us to be helpful and loving toward those who were weak or abnormal.

## Haarlem Inheritance

Grandfather Willem died when I was six months old, leaving Father his shop in Haarlem. We moved into the house, which wasn't very large, and poor Mother still didn't have her garden. She put some flowerpots on the flat roof and called this her yard. She had geraniums in clay pots, hanging fuchsia, and some ivy climbing the brick wall. She developed a roof garden long before the modern penthouse dwellers thought of such a thing.

Even in the "new" house in Haarlem, she could see only a small piece of the sky she loved. The roof became her "outdoors" when she became too weak to take her daily walks in the street.

During those first years of their marriage, the financial situation must have been very serious. Anna worked night and day to nurse Mother when she was ill and to care for four children. She earned the grand sum of one guilder (about thirty cents) a week. Father gave her this magnificent salary each Saturday, but often by the following Wednesday the finances would become so desperate that

Father would have to go to the kitchen and ask, "Anna, do you still have your guilder?"

Anna always had the guilder available, and it often bought the food for the family on that day. This was certainly "blessed money."

This was the beginning of my rich inheritance. When I remember my family life, I realize that my parents and my aunts had truly mastered the art of living. They enjoyed life and they loved children.

"We never laughed so much as when you children were small," Tante Anna often said.

In our hearts we must have stored some of the memory of laughter to be brought out in later years, when the sounds of happy voices were scarce in our beloved land.

# 2

## Five Is Not Too Young

In 1892, the year I was born, Holland was entering an exciting and important era. In a few years, Wilhelmina would be crowned queen at the tender age of eighteen. There were signs that the stability of the latter part of the nineteenth century would soon be rocked by the rattling of German swords. Foreign policy was being shaped around lines of power, as young Kaiser Wilhelm II ruled the country that later played such an important part in my life.

History in the making means nothing to a child, but it was a world event for me when Mother or Tante Anna pinched a guilder hard enough to squeeze out some sugar and butter for those fat little cookies I loved. The fragrance of baking would float from the iron stove into the shop and tantalize the customers just as it put us in a happy mood.

When I was five years old, I learned to read; I loved stories, particularly those about Jesus. He was a member of the ten Boom family—it was just as easy to talk to Him as it was to carry on a conversation with my mother and father, my aunts, or my brother and sisters. He was there.

One day my mother was watching me play house. In my little girl world of fantasy, she saw that I was pretending to call on a neighbor. I knocked on the make-believe door and waited . . . no one answered.

"Corrie, I know Someone who is standing at your door and knocking right now."

Was she playing a game with me? I know now that there was a preparation within my childish heart for that moment; the Holy Spirit makes us ready for acceptance of Jesus Christ, of turning our life over to Him.

"Jesus said that He is standing at the door, and if you invite Him in He will come into your heart," my mother continued. "Would you like to invite Jesus in?"

At that moment my mother was the most beautiful person in the whole world to me.

"Yes, Mama, I want Jesus in my heart."

So she took my little hand in hers and we prayed together. It was so simple, and yet Jesus Christ says that we all must come as children, no matter what our age, social standing, or intellectual background.

When Mother told me later about this experience, I recalled it clearly.

## But, You're So Little

Does a child of five really know what he's doing? Some people say that children don't have spiritual understanding—that we should wait until a child can "make up his mind for himself." I believe a child should be led, not left to wander.

Jesus became more real to me from that time on. Mother told me later that I began to pray for others, as young as I was.

The street behind our house was the Smedestraat. It was filled with saloons, and many of the happenings there were frightening to me. As I played outside, jumping rope, or joined with Nollie, my sister, in a game of *bikkelen* (ball and stones), I saw the police pick up these lurching, incoherent men as they slumped to the ground or slouched in a doorway, and take them into the police station.

I would stand before the *politie bureau* (police station) behind the Beje and watch the drunks being pushed in. It made me shiver. The building was made of dark red brick, and way at the top were turrets with small windows. Were those the cells, I wondered?

It was in that same police station years later that my father and all his children and a grandson were taken after being arrested for helping Jews escape from the German gestapo.

As a child, I would be so concerned for those arrested that I would run into the house sobbing, "Mother . . . I'm afraid those poor men are going to be hurt . . . they're so sick!"

Bless Mother's understanding. She would say, "Pray for them, Corrie."

And I would pray for the drunks. "Dear Jesus, please help those men . . . and Jesus, help all the people on the Smedestraat."

Many years later I spoke on a television station in Holland. I received a letter after the program that said, "My husband was especially interested because you told us that you had lived in Haarlem. He lived in a house on the Smedestraat. Three years ago he accepted the Lord Jesus as his Savior."

I read that letter and recalled the prayers of little Corrie. That man whose wife wrote me was one person I had prayed for seventy-six years before.

## Does He Listen?

At another time in my later years I was camping with a number of Haarlem girls. Around the campfire one evening, we were talking about the Lord and chatting about the pleasant events of the day.

"Do you know that I am a neighbor of yours?" one of the girls asked me. "I live in the Smedestraat."

"I lived there until five years ago," said another girl.

"My mother lived there," said a third.

We all began to laugh to discover that all eighteen of those girls, who were sleeping in the big camp tent, had lived on that street or their parents had lived there. They found it an amusing coincidence.

"Listen," I said, "I just remembered something that I had almost forgotten. When I was five or six years old, I used to pray every day for the people in the Smedestraat. The fact that we have been talking about Jesus and that God has even used me to reach some of your parents is an answer to the prayer of a little child. Never doubt whether God hears our prayers, even the unusual ones."

How often we think when a prayer is not answered that God has said no. Many times He has simply said, "Wait."

## The Future Comes Quickly

When we are very young the future is so hard to grasp. My father had one coming event that he mentioned in every prayer. It baffled me. I didn't want to ask in front of the entire family; I thought they might think I was foolish to ask about something I heard several times a day.

I waited until Father came upstairs to tuck me in; this was a time I could ask him anything.

"Papa, you always pray in every prayer, 'Let soon come that great day when Jesus Christ, Your beloved Son, comes on the clouds of heaven.' Why are you longing for that day?"

"Correman, remember when you saw the men drunk and fighting in the Smedestraat, and they were taken to the police station? The whole world is filled with fighting. You may see worse fighting in your lifetime than what you have seen on the street."

I hoped not. Fighting upset me.

"In the Bible," Papa continued, "we read that Jesus has promised to come to this world to make everything new. The world is now covered with hatred, but when Jesus returns, the world will be covered with the knowledge of God, like the water covers the bottom of the sea."

Thinking of that wonderful day, I knew why Papa prayed for it so often. "Oh, Papa, then everyone will know about Jesus! I'll be very happy when He comes."

## Let the Children Come

Decades later I was speaking to a group when I challenged parents to "bring your little ones to the Lord Jesus. He has said, 'Let the children come to me; the kingdom of God is theirs.'" (See Matthew 19:14.)

Then I told how I made a decision for Jesus when I was five years old.

After that talk I left the platform and went into a small room in the building where I found a father with two little boys, all on their knees. The father had an arm around both of those boys, and I moved back quietly while the man told the boys tenderly that they were not too young to ask Jesus to come into their hearts.

What a wonderful heritage those boys have, to know that their father cared enough about them to lead them to a knowledge of their heavenly Father!

Later I received a letter from a lady who told me the results in her life of that evening.

> I went home after that meeting and went directly to my little girl, Mary, who was in bed. She knew about the Lord because she had been to a Sunday school, but that night, in her bed, she gave her heart to Jesus.
>
> The next morning she said, "Oh, Mommy, I'm so happy that Jesus is now in my heart. He made me a child of God."
>
> Mary was singing the whole time before she went to school, and I was amazed that she sang many songs about heaven.
>
> My husband went to school to pick her up that day, and as he approached the schoolhouse, he noticed that a great many people were standing around, and there obviously must have been an accident. Then he saw what had happened.
>
> Mary was on the street, her little body crumpled like a rag doll. She was dead.

As I read that letter my eyes were so filled with tears that the words blurred.

> Mary had passed behind a big transport truck and had not seen another car, which was coming toward her from the other direction. She was killed immediately.
>
> My husband brought her little body home. He was in deep despair, but then he remembered the

songs Mary had sung that morning. I told him what
had happened the evening before, and right then, my
husband, who had never made a decision for the Lord
Jesus, accepted Him as his Savior.

On Mary's burial day many children of her class
came to the Lord.

I sat for a long time with that letter on my lap, realizing that I must have a new sense of urgency to talk to parents about the joy of leading their children to the Lord.
What a wonderful assurance Mary's parents had, to know
that someday they would be with her again.

During some of my talks I have often repeated this
little poem:

**Safe?**
Said a precious little laddie,
To his father one bright day,
"May I give myself to Jesus,
Let Him wash my sins away?"

O, my son, but you're so little,
Wait until you older grow,
Bigger folks 'tis true, do need Him,
But little folk are safe, you know.

Said the father to his laddie,
As a storm was coming on,
"Are the sheep all safely sheltered,
Safe within the fold, my son?"

"All the big ones are, my father,

But the lambs, I let them go,
For I didn't think it mattered,
Little ones are safe, you know."

*Author Unknown*

## Praying for Crazy Thys

As a child in Haarlem I prayed for a man most people avoided. His nickname was Gekke Thys (Crazy Thys), and he was the town tramp, an idiot. I pitied him and when I was five or six years old started to talk about this to the Lord.

How curious the little minds of children are. Was it my mother or one of my aunts who gave me the advice to cast my burden on the Lord in prayer? Or did the Lord Himself give me this motivation?

Every prayer in the evening and in the morning ended with this request: "And Lord, be with all the people in the Smedestraat and also Gekke Thys."

My sister, Nollie, was only a year and a half older than I, but she seemed so much wiser. I remember walking with her through the Smedestraat one day and stopping to watch a crowd of children surrounding someone they were taunting and teasing. As we inched closer to the others, wanting to know what was happening but a bit afraid of getting involved in something that looked so mean, we realized that poor old Crazy Thys was standing in the middle of the circle, confusion and hurt showing in his face.

I was so full of pity for poor Thys and angry at the cruel children that I shouted, "You leave him alone, do you hear!"

The children stopped at my bold challenge. Thys looked for his defender and saw a little girl, less than half his size. Suddenly he walked toward me and stooped down. I could smell the unpleasant odor of his unwashed clothes and matted beard. He put his hand under my chin and kissed me on both cheeks.

Nollie was shocked! She grabbed my hand and pulled me home as fast as we could run. Down the Smedestraat, into the alley that ran beside our house, and through the side door we raced.

"Aunty, someone . . . hurry! That dirty old *Gekke Thys* kissed Corrie. Let's wash her cheeks!"

My face was so thoroughly washed I was afraid my skin would fall off. I heard someone say, "Such dangerous tramps shouldn't be allowed to go so freely in the streets."

Stinging from the rebuke as well as the face scrubbing, I went to my mother. "Mama, why was it so bad that *Gekke Thys* kissed me? He's such a poor unhappy man. Everybody makes fun of him."

Mother took me into her bed and talked quietly with me as I nestled against her soft shoulder. She said, "Correman, it's good that you have pity for this man. The Lord Jesus gives you love for *Gekke Thys* and for the drunken men in the Smedestraat. Jesus loves sinners, but before they are going to love Him, these men can be very bad. It's wise to keep a little distance. But there's one great thing you and I can do—and you are doing that already—pray faithfully for them."

Shortly after that incident *Gekke Thys* disappeared from the streets. I don't know how the Lord worked in his life, but a deep concern for the feebleminded was fostered in me.

## Fear No Evil . . . Except

A child is not fearless, contrary to what his parents may think at times. A child is often a bundle of unexpressed fears, unknown terrors, and shadowy worries. I was afraid of the doctor's office, my family's leaving me, and the mystery of death.

Nollie's nightgown was my contact with security. We slept in the same bed, and I can remember clinging to Nollie's nightgown as long as she would allow me. Poor Nollie, when she would try to turn, she would be anchored by my little fist clasping her tightly.

One time Mother took Nollie and me to visit a woman whose baby had died. I wished Nollie had been allowed to wear her nightgown on that journey, because I needed desperately to hang on to it.

We climbed a narrow staircase and entered the poorly furnished room of one of Mama's "lame ducks" (the name we children had given to her protégés). Although we often did not have sufficient money for ourselves, Mother always found someone who was in greater need.

In that shabby little room was a crib with a baby inside. It didn't move at all and its skin was very white. Nollie stood next to the crib and touched the baby's cheek.

"Feel that," she said to me. "It's so cold."

I touched the little hand and then ran to my mother and buried my face in her lap. I had touched death for the first time, and it seemed that the impression of cold remained with me for hours and hours.

When we returned home, I ran up the narrow stairs to my bedroom and leaned against the antique chest of drawers. There was an enormous fear in my heart—almost terror. In my imagination, I pictured the future in which I saw myself all alone, my family gone, and myself left desolate. My family was my security, but that day I saw death and knew that they could die too. I had never thought about it before.

The dinner bell rang downstairs, and I was so grateful to go to the big oval table and get warm again and feel the security of being with my family. I thought how stupid the grown-ups would think I was if I told them about the fear that was still in my heart.

I ate dinner quietly that night, which was not easy when you are in the midst of such a lively family. Our dinner table spilled over with conversation.

After dinner Father took the Bible, as he always did, and began to read the lines from Psalm 46:2. "Therefore will not we fear, though the earth be removed, and though the mountains be carried into the midst of the sea" (KJV).

I sat up straight in my chair and stared at my father. I didn't know much about mountains, living in flat, flat Holland, but I certainly knew a lot about fear. I thought Papa must have known exactly what my problem was that night.

My faith in Papa, and in the words he read from the Bible, was absolute. If they said not to fear, then God would take care of it. I felt secure again.

# 3

## From Small Beginnings

My doll, Casperina, and I were going to have a party! Mama and Tante Anna were cooking, and I watched their long skirts bustle past me from my perch on the footstool beneath the table. This was a wonderful place to play, safe and secure beneath the red and black tablecloth.

My friend was named after my father, but the resemblance ended there. I loved her very much, but dragging her up and down the stairs of the Beje had left her with a few fingers missing and a slightly cracked head. Oh, my, why couldn't she look like Nollie's doll, who was immaculately dressed and didn't have a scratch on her china face? Poor Casperina, she would never be in the same society with Emma, Betsie's doll, who was named after the mother of the queen.

"Never mind, Casperina," I whispered to her in the shelter of our little house beneath the table, "Jesus loves you, and so do I."

When I was especially happy, I would sing a little song that Tante Jans had composed:

'k Zou zoo graag eens komen, Heiland,
In dat heerlijk Vaderhuis.

31

(I should just like to come, Savior,
In the beautiful Father-house.)

However, instead of singing to *come* I substituted to peek, combining my words with a mischievous look around the fat table leg.

Tante Anna laughed at me. "Corrie, you'd better not let Tante Jans hear you change the words in her songs. When she writes 'I should like to come to heaven,' that's what she means."

*Some things grown-ups don't understand,* I thought. I meant that it would be great fun just to look around for a moment in heaven, where I knew I would spend my future. I just wanted a little peek; after all, my father-house right here on the Barteljorisstraat was all the heaven I wanted right then.

I clutched Casperina's three-fingered hand in mine and whispered, "We'll just stay in our own secret place, where no one will ever—ever—scold us for anything."

## A Time to Uproot

A time comes when all children, even a little Dutch girl with her jaw set and her black-stockinged legs rigid upon the staircase, must leave their father's house for a time. I was born with my feet slightly turned in, a defect that the doctor said would cure itself with time and growth.

"Don't worry," he told Mama and Papa, "when she is about sixteen, she will become vain enough to turn her toes the right way."

However, when I turned my toes in even more and

tightened my fingers in a knuckle-whitening grip on the railing, I meant business.

"I'm not going to school. I know how to read; I can learn arithmetic from Papa, and Casperina needs me at home."

There. *That* was settled.

"Of course you're not going to school alone, Corrie. I am going to walk with you."

Papa bent over me, his beard tickling the top of my head, and one by one loosened my fingers on the railing. With the release of each finger, I howled a bit louder. By the time Papa had my hand in his, he was almost dragging me down the street toward school. I thought my hand would break—just like Casperina's—and then it would be impossible for me to go to school.

It must have taken great dignity for Papa, with his immaculate suit and erect carriage, to struggle past the homes and shops of his friends with a red-faced child announcing her objections to the entire world.

I knew Father was not angry, but his will was law. I had to obey.

When we arrived at the school, I saw a little boy being carried into Master Robyns's classroom in his father's arms. (At least I was walking!) He was crying lustily, even louder than I was. He looked so ugly that I felt sorry for him. But what about me? I realized how I must look to others and stopped abruptly.

Papa released my hand; my fingers weren't broken at all—only my heart was slightly injured. However, when Papa kissed me gently on the cheek, bringing the familiar fragrance of cigars and cologne, he assured me that when school was over, he would be waiting at home, and I knew

I would find that blessed security I needed in the shelter of his arms.

God was teaching a little lesson in a small life, because sixty-seven years later, He reminded me of my fingers on the railing.

I was in a room of *Zonneduin,* a house in Holland that some friends and I had established first for ex-prisoners who had been in concentration camps, and later for any person who needed nursing and rest. I had been traveling so much and was tired—tired of strange beds and different food, tired of dressing for breakfast, tired of new people and new experiences. I liked this very luxurious house with its large rooms and decided to stay and enjoy the comfortable life in Holland, although I knew that God didn't agree with my decision.

Most of the furniture in the entire house was mine, but there was one room in particular that reminded me of the happy family life of my past. It was a room that held my treasures: photographs of those I loved, mementos of my family during the years before. Every picture was like the railing on the stairs. My hands grasped the past and tried to hold on, but my heavenly Father's hands were stronger.

I left the house for a while for some speaking engagements, intending to return to my old room and settle in for good. However, when I came back to *Zonneduin* some weeks later, my pictures were down and the strange belongings of someone else were on the bed.

My friends had not known of my personal decision to return to this room; my irregular life, my coming and going unexpectedly, was difficult for those who had to manage the big family of patients and staff in an orderly way.

But I decided to stay, and that was settled!

My heavenly Father spoke to me, "Only obey me, Corrie. I'll hold your hand. It is My will that you leave your room. Later you will thank Me for this experience. You do not see it, but this is one of My great blessings for you."

Father's hand was firm, but I knew His love.

I packed up my suitcase again and left for the United States. How the Lord blessed my time there. Meetings began to grow in size, and when I saw people come from darkness into light, from bondage into liberation, I began to see the pattern. I could praise my Father that His hands were stronger than mine.

## Blue Stones Can Hurt!

School life did not prove to be as horrible as I thought. I can still remember the sensation of victory when I worked an arithmetic problem and discovered that the final figure was what it was supposed to be. However, my mind was not always so attentive to details. I was a daydreamer, carrying my fantasies into a world where everyone needed an expensive new watch, and every day was a walk on the dunes with the sunshine warming my cheeks.

The headmaster of our school was a strict taskmaster, insisting upon obedience and discipline without question. He had warned all the children not to step on the "blue stone," which was a small square stone slightly higher than the rest in the outer yard. I was not paying attention to his instructions and stepped on the stone.

Instantly my face was smarting from a sharp slap on my cheek. I can still feel the shame of it, after all these years, for I don't believe the people at home had ever slapped my face. A color photoplate was impressed upon my mind, which has never faded. The tears covered my face, but I could see the girl who stood in front of me who wore a red dress and a white apron; there was a green door on the garden gate, and the colors all blended with the blazing eyes of Mr. Loran, the headmaster.

I couldn't wait to get home that day. Before I opened the door my cries had overpowered the sound of the bell, which announced any visitors to the shop.

Mama took me on her lap and comforted me; and when I had quieted, Papa held me in his arms as he did when I was a baby. I can still feel the sensation of safety as I put my head upon his shoulder. What a security to have a refuge when life is really hard!

Forty-five years passed after the blue-stone incident. The gestapo had arrested me, and I was being asked the location of the secret room in which I had hidden four Jews and two underground workers. I realized that if I told, it would mean prison and possibly death for the six people who were there, so I didn't tell. The interrogator slapped me on the face, and at the same moment I recalled the backyard of the school, the angry headmaster, and Mother and Father's comforting help.

"Lord Jesus, cover me!" I cried.

"If you mention that name, I'll murder you!" shouted the man interrogating me. But his hand stopped in midair and he couldn't beat me any longer.

What a security to have a refuge when life is really hard!

## In Dat Vaderhuis (In That Father-house)

Our house was not very big, but it had wide open doors. I don't think that many guests who came to the Beje ever realized what a struggle it was to make both ends meet. As Mother said, "We must turn every penny twice before we spend it."

We didn't feel that we were poor, however, and indeed we weren't. The words "we can't afford it" were not a part of our thinking, because as children we knew something about the status of family finances and didn't ask for what we knew was impossible.

Many lonesome people found a place with us, where there was music, humor, interesting conversations, and always room for one more at the oval dinner table. Oh, it's true, the soup may have been a bit watery when too many unexpected guests came, but it didn't really matter.

Mother loved guests. Her lovely blue eyes would brighten, and she would pat her dark hair into place when she knew we would be squeezing another visitor around our table—already bursting with four children, three aunts, herself, and Papa. With a flourish she would place a little box on the table, and spreading her arms wide, she would say to our visitor, "You are welcome in our house, and because we are grateful for your coming, we will add a penny to the blessing box for our missionaries."

Years afterward on my trips around the world, when I have been dependent upon the hospitality of others, I believe that I have enjoyed the reward for the open doors and hearts of our home. Here on earth I have enjoyed a "house with many mansions."

I often think of the verse that says, "Cast thy bread

upon the waters: for thou shalt find it after many days"
(Ecclesiastes 11:1 KJV).

### Corrie, Stand Still!

Although money was scarce, the outside world thought
we were wealthy. Every member of the family dressed
neatly and well. At least—almost everyone. Mother made
most of our clothes, until the burden became too much,
and Miss Anna van der Weyden, the seamstress, came in
to help.

Clothes to me were just something to keep me covered and warm. The endless fittings for a new dress and
the inevitable pricks from countless pins were torture to
my restless body.

"Corrie, come here, dear," Mother would call in the
tone I knew was meant to be another torturous session
trying on clothes.

"If I don't finish this homework, Mama, Master
Robyns will make me stand in the corner."

"Corrie!"

There was no escape. I knew if I didn't subject myself
to trying on a new dress that Mama was making, I would
probably be assigned next time to Miss van der Weyden,
and her clothes didn't fit as well as Mama's. The whole
process was such a bore, and there was no way I could
look like Nollie or Betsie anyhow. I just preferred to be
me. However, I was a ten Boom and must not bring
shame to the family name!

Mother had such a marvelous sense of humor, and
having been a kindergarten teacher before her marriage,
we profited by her practical knowledge of child

psychology. She knew that praising my appearance would not provide me with motivation for my self-esteem. However, when she said, "Correman, you are such a bright girl . . . I'm sure Master Robyns calls on you often in class. You do want to look nice when you stand up to recite, don't you?" then she would strike a responsive chord, for I was eager to learn and have recognition in school.

I stood still for Mama, but only briefly. There was so much to do, so many things to learn, so much to live. I had a built-in sense of urgency to cram all that life and love could offer into each precious day.

# 4

---

## The Many Ages of Love

Children need the wisdom of their elders; the aging need the encouragement of a child's exuberance.

Wisdom and exuberance lived side by side in the Beje, a house filled with the varied personalities of the old and the young.

### Tante Bep (Alone in the Crowd)

Children's nurses in the rich houses of Holland were very lonely. They were not at home in the kitchen with the servant girls (who thought the nurses had privileges that they didn't enjoy), and they were not at home in the drawing room with the master and mistress of the house. Consequently, they frequently became bitter with their circumstances of not belonging in any niche of society. Tante Bep was a children's nurse, going from job to job and becoming more unhappy each year.

She was the oldest of Mother's sisters, and one of the reasons (I realize now) that my mother was very skilled in the art of tact. Mother usually had to steer a smooth course in our family with all of the aunts and their individual views on education and discipline; she knew how to bring the ship between the rocks.

When Tante Bep became too weak to work as a nurse, Father and Mother took her in. She had the same big, beautiful eyes like Mother, but the expression was very unhappy. She was quarrelsome about everything. There was the issue of the coffee, for instance. She told Tante Anna, "I'm the only one in this house who can make coffee." Now if there's one thing that was important in our house it was a good cup of coffee. Tante Anna would shift her apron around her ample waist, clear her throat with gusto, and say, "Bep, if you think your coffee is so good, you may just take over all the cooking from now on."

"Anna," Mother would say with her soft smile and gentle persuasion, "we couldn't exist without your fine cooking—and Bep, I know your coffee is excellent too; so perhaps you would like to make it your way on Tuesdays and Thursdays."

It was such a small house, it was impossible to avoid Tante Bep, but I tried because I didn't like to be compared to the Waller children. The last place she worked before coming to live with us was with the Wallers, and I thought they must have been angels who had their halos polished every day.

The Waller children were always neat. The Waller children never ran in the house. I didn't like to tell Tante Bep anything, because she might say, "The Waller children would never say such a thing."

Mother always soothed my insulted feelings by telling me, "Tante Bep complained about the Waller children when she was caring for them. Love her for what she is, Correman, and remember that she has had a very lonely sort of a life."

### Tante Jans (That's That!)

"Corrie, close the door . . . my feet are cold and I'll be sick with all the drafts in this house."

Tante Jans was always concerned about her health and made us very conscious of her needs. She had a diet that was different from the usual fare of the rest of the family; as a child, I sometimes thought it would be interesting to be sick and have my own trays of food and special attention.

Her rooms were special too. Mother and Father had given her more floor space than the rest of the family because Tante Jans had a great deal of furniture to fill the rooms she occupied upstairs.

Her husband had been a well-known minister in Rotterdam, and she had worked faithfully beside him in the church. They had no children, and it was a great loss in her life when he died before she was forty years old. After his death, it was clear that her place was to be in our house.

Tante Jans was not a woman to curl up with grief, and as soon as she had become established in her new quarters, she began all of her many activities that contributed to our buzzing household.

She was a poetess, an authoress, and an unusually good speaker. She started a monthly paper for girls, wrote books with a gospel message, organized clubs for young women, and even began a club for soldiers.

One time Tante Jans swept into the house, pulling the scarf off her mouth, and proclaimed, "There are soldiers wandering around the streets of Haarlem with idle minds and mischievous thoughts. I am going to start a club for soldiers."

*That's that!* It was settled. When Tante Jans made one of her announcements, the wheels were set in motion. Before we knew what had happened, our house began to look like a military installation. They would come alone or in pairs, young men who disliked the street life and were looking for the simple warmth of a home. One sergeant she met on a streetcar was a great musician. When he saw the harmonium that Tante Jans had against the wall of her room, he sat down and began to play, making the thin walls of the house quiver with each cre-scendo of volume.

Tante Jans folded her hands and listened intently to the talented soldier. She decided that Nollie and I should have him give us music lessons.

Even if we had not enjoyed music, we would have learned because Tante Jans decreed it. Soon I could play hymns well enough to join in the meetings and accompany the singing. It taught me at a very young age not to be self-conscious in the presence of men—although I don't think that was the intent of Tante Jans.

Some people have the gift of raising money by convincing others of the worth of a project, and this was one of Tante Jans's special talents. One afternoon she had a tea and invited some wealthy women she knew to come to her rooms. We scurried around, rubbing her silver tea set until it glistened and making sure everything was immaculate for the occasion.

I peeked out the window and watched the ladies arrive, swishing into the house with their long dresses underlined with full petticoats. How could they possibly walk and maneuver the narrow stairway with all those skirts? I had a hard time just keeping my feet in front of me! *It must be a burden to be rich and have to dress in such fancy clothes,* I thought.

Evidently Tante Jans was convincing, for in a short time she had enough money to build a military home. When it was finished and filled with soldiers, she went twice a week to give Bible studies.

Tante Jans didn't move with the times; she marched to her own beat. Her outspoken ideas on behavior, clothes, and theology were constant abrasives on the surface of our family relationships.

When I was a child, I thought Tante Jans was very rich because she was a minister's widow and received a small, regular pension. Sometimes she would have an unexpected donation, and we would all share her joy. However, when she bought clothing for us it could be embarrassing—especially for Nollie and Betsie who had their own very distinctive tastes.

"Oh, dear," Betsie would say as she turned to give us the effect of a drab gray dress Tante Jans had given her. "Do you think she would mind if I put some lace around the neck—or maybe a pink sash at the waist?"

"Betsie, if you think that's bad, just look at this hat," Nollie would groan as she pulled a bonnet on backward, sending us all into suppressed giggles. Tante Jans's taste in hats was somewhere between the style of a servant girl and that of a great-grandmother. Nollie was very fashion-conscious, and the gifts of stodgy clothes were a challenge to her ingenuity.

I didn't care about my appearance; I accepted all she gave me and consequently received the most hats and dresses. During the First World War most of Tante Jans's income stopped; it was dependent upon gifts of people who were having a financial struggle themselves. I remember she was surprised by an unexpected gift of fifty guilders (about eighteen dollars) and quickly gathered her muffler and umbrella to go shopping. When she returned, we thought something amazing must have happened, because she had forgotten to button her coat to the top. The sight of Tante Jans with face flushed and scarf loose was as uncommon as seeing the queen riding in a streetcar!

"Come in everyone . . . I have something to show you." We all followed her into her room, and she spread her packages on the sofa and began to distribute them with suppressed excitement. There was a warm blanket for Mother, a coat for me (black and shapeless, but practical), a blouse for Tante Anna, and cakes for the whole family. Any sweets were rare for us, reserved for birthdays and very special occasions.

I found out later that she had spent more than seventy guilders on us. I believe she was one of the richest persons I have known, for she knew how to give to others.

## Tante Anna (Sheltering Apron)

Tante Anna, stocky, practical, unsentimental, was our substitute mother whenever Mother was too ill to care for us. She ruled over her little basement kitchen like one of Tante Jans's sergeants over his platoon. She was firm and hardworking, but overflowing with love for Mother, Father, and all the children. When I was very young, I would stand beside her in our basement kitchen and lick the bowl of something she had been making. I watched the legs of the people passing by the kitchen window, for that was all we could see from beneath the street level. I began to wonder about all the people in the gigantic world outside.

"Tante Anna, where do babies come from?" I asked.

She stirred the *alle haphetzelfde* a bit and answered carefully, "Well, Corrie, when a baby is too small and weak to live in the cold world, there is a place underneath a mother's heart where it is kept warm and can grow, until it is strong enough to stand the cold in the big world."

I could understand that. It seemed like a very good plan of the Lord's.

My question answered in a simple manner, I went on to the more important matters of life, such as investigating with my finger the inside of another bowl. This one contained a special treat—*allusion*, which was a dessert made with stiffened egg whites and flavored with lemon and sugar. There was more air than substance, but good for a big family.

Tante Anna was a good cook, stretching a little far. She would cook a stew on the big, black coal stove until most of the vegetables all blended into each other. The *alle haphetzelfde* meant "every bite the same," and I know it was a real surprise and a treat when we encountered a bit of meat.

She had her club work too, and her concern for others reached into the homes of the wealthy who employed servant girls. Every Wednesday and Sunday evening a group of them would come to a club room and bring their sewing and embroidery work. Tante Anna taught them gospel songs and gave them a Bible study. When one of "her girls" went the wrong way, Tante Anna became ill. Her face would become puffy and swell, and we didn't have to ask; we knew that she had received a piece of bad news.

"Tante Anna, who was it this time?" we would ask.

She would take her apron and try to hide her blotchy face. "It was Betty," she would say, dabbing at her eyes. "She wasn't strong enough in the Lord . . . she ran off with

Hans . . . he's had two wives before this!" She would become as distressed as any mother would over a wayward child.

"Anna," Father would say, "you must not bear this yourself. Cast your worries upon the Lord."

## Nollie (Mijn Moedertje)

Nollie was physically the strongest of the three girls in the family. I considered her my elder, although she was only a year and a half older than I. Even when she was a little child, she felt responsible for me; she was my *moedertje* (little mother). As a toddler, whenever she drank water she brought a cup for me too. I had to drink even if I wasn't thirsty. After all, Nollie knew best. I was shy and she was not; she voiced her needs and views. I waited.

One time, when we were very young, Nollie and I were out for a walk when a man on a bicycle knocked us down right in front of our house. Covered with mud and shocked, we ran into the sitting room, loudly declaring our presence.

Nollie screamed and everyone came running, brushing her hair out of her eyes, wiping off the dirt, and kissing away the tears. I stood in the corner, watching all the commotion and wondering when I should take my turn screaming—after Nollie was through, of course. I knew my time to be comforted would come.

Suddenly Mother said, "*Hemeltje!* [Little Heaven!] Come look at Corrie."

Everyone stopped and for the first time realized that I was standing in the corner of the room, big tears making muddy rivers down my cheeks. Finally I was given the attention of the grown-ups.

The little alley beside our house was the locale of many events in our lives. There wasn't much room for playing in our overcrowded house, so the alley was our yard, our recreation room, and our schoolhouse of life. Once Nollie met a little boy named Sammy Staal. I think there must have been something wrong with his heart, for his skin had a bluish color and his nose was always red. He was unable to walk and propelled himself in a wheelchair. Nollie made friends with him, and encouraged by Mother, she would push him for hours and hours while the rest of the children were playing active games. When he died, Nollie was heartbroken.

Nollie's grief was probably a shared feeling. Even when we were very young, we knew that our problems were never too small for the grown-ups; there were many ways and many ages of love under one Dutch roof.

# 5

## Winking Angels

Secrets are for children, and promises are like soap bubbles—easy to make, easy to break. The one time I tried to keep a secret from Mama, my little deception was uncovered. I talked in my sleep.

I was very young, perhaps eight or nine, and very flattered that Richard would ask me to go for a walk through the dunes. He was the nephew of our minister and quite grown up—a teenager.

However, I was not prepared for an act of boyish curiosity that surprised and shamed me at the same time. We had reached a valley where we could not be seen, and suddenly he pulled me close to him and started to do very strange things. Even without previous warnings from protective parents, I knew this was wrong.

I pulled away from him, flushing with childish indignation, and stamped my foot. "Richard, you stop that. Mama would think that's dirty!"

Richard looked frightened but defiant. "She isn't here . . . and you mustn't tell."

"Mama isn't here, but Jesus is, and I'm sure He doesn't think it's right."

Richard was defeated. He stopped immediately and

said, "Promise me never to tell anyone what I tried to do, especially your mother?"

I thought this over for a while. After all, he was Richard, and a very important person in my eyes.

"Well, I guess so . . . I promise."

As we walked back home, he told me some very nice stories and I forgot about the incident.

At least I thought I forgot about it!

The next day I was ill and had a fever. I talked about the walk on the dunes but wasn't conscious of what I had said. After the fever was gone, Mama asked me what had happened with Richard.

"A promise is a promise, Mama, and I said I wouldn't tell anybody in the world."

"Correman, never forget that Jesus is always with you. Every morning I ask Him to keep you and all of my children within His constant care. In the evening, I thank Him that He sent His angels to guard you. Now you and I will pray together."

I remember Mother folded her soft hands around mine when she prayed. I thought how wonderful it was that she asked Jesus to guard me. She prayed, "Thank You, Jesus, that You never leave my Correman alone . . . thank You that You protected her during her walk on the dunes. Please lay Your hand on Richard . . . show him how wrong he was and that You are willing to make him a good clean boy."

How did she know about Richard? I wondered if mothers know everything. Oh, well, never mind . . . Jesus knows, Mama knows, and everything is all right.

## Dutch Mischief Makers

I was no little angel. Mischief was my middle name, and Dot, my cousin and best friend, was my willing partner. Her father, Uncle Arnold, was the usher, or verger, of St. Bavo's, the magnificent Gothic cathedral that dominates the center of Haarlem. Its cavernous interior provided endless hours of imaginary play. In the banks (or pews) with their enclosed rows of seats, shut off from the aisles by half doors, a child could have a private house. We could be pirates, hiding in our caves, or storekeepers in our offices; we could run a school or own a sweet shop.

The pulpit was out of bounds. We were not allowed to go there; that wasn't proper or respectful. It seemed quite awesome to a small child, because the chair in the pulpit doesn't stand on the ground. It is held up by the bronze wings of an eagle. The font in front of the pulpit is supported by three brass snakes, and that was enough to keep us away without being told.

Our voices would echo in the stone interior, adding intrigue to our games. Sometimes Uncle Arnold would have to hush our exuberance.

"Children, children, there are graves beneath our feet. Step softly."

The position of usher carried the privilege of living within the cathedral grounds. Uncle Arnold's family had a cozy little house just off the side entrance to the church. I always loved going in through the narrow passageway surrounded by beautiful blue Dutch tiles.

Living within the cathedral didn't make Dot any holier. If I didn't dream up a prank, she would.

We were in the same grade in school and usually walked together to our classes. I was comfortable with

Dot because we were on the same level of academic achievement, which was toward the bottom of the class. Whenever we had difficulty with our homework, we asked Josien van Paassen to help us. She was not only bright but also owned a bicycle. A winning combination. Her father was a minister with a regular monthly income, but the earnings of a watchmaker went up and down like the weights on the grandfather clock.

One morning Dot called for me on the way to school, and she was unusually excited. "Corrie, come here, look what I found."

She handed me a dime that was broken in half; the coin had probably been run over by a carriage, and the two pieces were wedged on the cobblestones just waiting for a little girl to pick them up. A dime was a great deal of money to us; it could buy ten pieces of candy at the sweet-shop on the Begynestraat. Such a rare and wonderful treat!

We skipped off to school, neither one of us admitting that we thought we were going to do anything wrong, and ordered our candies from the jolly lady who owned the shop. Dot slipped the two parts of the dime to me and I placed them on the counter, then made a very fast retreat out the door. We were running toward school when we heard the bell of the shop door ring and the owner call, "Girls . . . girls . . . come back . . . !"

I grabbed Dot's hand and we ran a little faster, my feet having their usual problem of keeping up with my own momentum. We felt so guilty and for weeks avoided going by the candy store. The candy didn't taste very good either, and in later years when I read this Proverb I thought about that childish caper. "Bread obtained by falsehood is sweet to a man, but afterward his mouth will be filled with gravel" (Proverbs 20:17). Can candy really taste like gravel?

Another time Dot and I made some solid snowballs and put them in our pockets. It was so cold they didn't melt but formed hard balls just the right size for mittened hands to grasp and throw. We were walking through the Kruisstraat behind three dignified men, who were loudly discussing their problems. I winked at Dot, and we reached into our pockets, drew out our ammunition, took aim, and fired. The top hats flew into the snowy streets, and two sweet little girls raced to pick them up.

"Here you are, sir," I said with a serious face and very polite demeanor, as I brushed the snow carefully off the hat. Dot picked up the second hat and handed it to one gentleman who had a very bald, cold head. He fitted the hat on his head and said, "Thank you, young ladies," as he looked around to see who the rascals were who committed such a crime.

## Hats Off

Not all my episodes with hats went unpunished, however.

The director of our school was a very strict man, not the type of person who would tolerate misbehavior from his students. Father had helped Mr. van Lyden start the Christian educational institution, and because of this assistance we didn't pay to attend it, a fact that was a great help to the ten Boom family. When the school was new, many of the disciplinary problem children from other areas were sent there, and several times Mr. van Lyden had to send them back to the schools they had attended previously.

I was shocked when a student was expelled. Just imagine how humiliating it was for the parents to have their child sent away from school for bad behavior!

I must have been about ten years old when this occurred. I sat at my desk, gazing out the window, watching the wind swirl the dust on the playground. I was thinking about the new hat Tante Jans had given me, a large blue and white sailor, which I hated just because it was a hat. The teacher stepped out of the room and an idea flashed into my mind.

"Listen, everyone," I said to the class, "I have a brilliant idea. Exactly at two o'clock we'll all put on our hats or caps. We can smuggle them under the desks so Mr. van Ree won't see them. I've got a watch and I'll give the sign."

The room of sixty ten-year-olds crackled with excitement, and I was the leader. The fact that I had a watch made me very important, because I was the only one in the class who had one.

Two o'clock arrived and the classroom was very quiet. We were working out arithmetic problems in silence, and the teacher looked from one to another, distrusting our unusually good behavior.

I was sitting toward the front of the class and, after giving the signal, I took my hat from under my desk and put it on. I didn't hear a thing in back of me. I looked around and to my horror saw that no one else had the nerve to follow my example, except Jan Vixeboxe who sat way in the back of the room. When my eyes returned to the teacher, he was staring right at me, furiously glaring from humorless eyes. There was terror in the atmosphere.

"Go to the headmaster at once, Corrie ten Boom!" he commanded.

Oh, no, not the headmaster! That was Mr. van Lyden, and he expelled students for infraction of the rules.

I slipped from behind my desk, pulling off my hat as I left the room. In the hallway I opened the coat closet and ducked in, hiding myself in a dark corner behind the coats. I don't know how many miserable hours I spent there, but it seemed like an eternity before the bell rang and I ran out ahead of the rest of the students.

I expected to be dismissed, just as the problem pupils from other schools had been. I thought of all the shame I would bring to Mama and Papa, of all they would have to go through because of my misdeed. How I loved them! I thought of all the care they had given me, of the difficulties we had as a result of sickness and lack of money. We were such a close-knit family that we always shared joys and sorrows, and now this! Dismissed from the school my father had helped organize!

At the supper table that night I was so quiet Mama thought I was sick. I went upstairs early and crept into bed, pulling the comforter under my chin. I told Nollie everything that had happened.

"Why don't you ask forgiveness of God?" she suggested.

"I've already done that . . . but do you think He will arrange it so that I won't be sent away from school?"

I asked Nollie the deep questions that were puzzling me, because she was almost twelve! Certainly she would know all the answers.

"I don't know," Nollie replied, "but do you remember that boring psalm that Papa read at the table, where every sixth or seventh verse were the same words? 'Then they cried unto the LORD in their trouble, and he saved them out of their distresses'" (Psalm 107 KJV).

For the first time since the hats-off incident I began to cheer up. "Why couldn't we do the same?"

We "cried unto the Lord" and then fell asleep. The next morning Nollie shook me awake and told me her wonderful idea. We had a little monthly missionary magazine that I delivered to several people as my special work in evangelizing the world. Mr. van Lyden was one of the subscribers. Nollie suggested, "You must manage in some way to go to the headmaster and personally bring him the mission magazine for this month. It can't do any harm, and perhaps it will do some good."

That morning, with my heart pounding right through my best school dress and a very pious expression on my face, I went to the headmaster's room and handed him the paper. He looked at it and then at me. The pause took a hundred years and the silence hurt my ears. He didn't have much of a sense of humor, but I believe the corners of his mouth turned up just a little bit.

He cleared his throat, tapped the desk with his pencil, and said, "Corrie ten Boom, I don't think you behaved as a very good Christian girl yesterday."

That was all I ever heard about my crime. The Lord saved me from my distress.

## Mice in the Manuscript

When I was about twelve, I decided that I wanted to be a writer. I curled up on my bed, pad of paper on my lap, and wove a wonderful fantasy about the adventures of Nollie, Josien, Dot, and all of Dot's brothers and sisters on a holiday without our parents. It was a beautiful story, filled with more adventure than Dickens and more vivid character sketches than Louisa May Alcott. How famous I would be!

Betsie shattered my dreams. She came into the room and asked, "What's that?"

It seemed quite obvious to me. "It's a book I'm writing," I answered as smugly as a sister seven years younger could reply to the ridiculous question of a grown-up.

Betsie seldom voiced any words of discouragement, but this time she said, "How foolish . . . you can't write a book."

*I just won't show anyone my book anymore,* I thought. So I hid it in the attic and forgot the priceless manuscript for several months.

When I remembered later to take the papers out of their secret niche, there was only one-tenth of this potential best-seller left. The rest was eaten by the mice. I was so disappointed that I decided never to write a book again.

## The Shadow of His Wings

My security was assured in many ways as a child. Every night I would go to the door of my room in my nightie and call out, "Papa, I'm ready for bed." He would come to my room and pray with me before I went to sleep. I can remember that he always took time with us, and he would tuck the blankets around my shoulders very carefully, with his own characteristic precision. Then he would put his hand gently on my face and say, "Sleep well, Corrie . . . I love you."

I would be very, very still, because I thought that if I moved I might lose the touch of his hand; I wanted to feel it until I fell asleep.

Many years later in a concentration camp in Germany, I sometimes remembered the feeling of my father's hand on my face. When I was lying beside Betsie on a wretched, dirty mattress in that dehumanizing prison, I would say, "Oh, Lord, let me feel Your hand upon me . . . may I creep under the shadow of Your wings."

In the midst of that suffering was my heavenly Father's security.

## Reach as High as You Can

My desire to please my papa was one of the basic motivations of my life. I remember when I was walking home from school, there was a very dirty wall I passed every day. It was full of flies, and during the warm weather one of my games was to run my hand along the wall and try to catch a fly. When the challenge had been met, I would release it and try for the next catch.

One day when I was busy with this messy game, I heard a familiar voice behind me, "Now isn't this a joy to meet my youngest daughter here on the street."

I was suddenly very embarrassed about how dirty I was, for Papa was so immaculate and well dressed that I didn't dare put my hand in his. He never mentioned my appearance, just walked along chatting about the visit to Mrs. de Vries and his talk with the servant girl about the Lord, until we arrived inside the Beje.

"I'm home, Cor," he'd call to Mama. Then he turned to me and said, "And I know, Corrie, that you're going to wash your hands before you see your mother."

Such a small thing, but I remember the shame of being so dirty in Papa's presence.

We were always challenged to do our best. When Papa took a watch apart and put it back together again, it was a task he performed without regard to the owner's social status or wealth. He taught us that it wasn't important what you think, or even what other people think, but what God thinks about the job you have done.

When Nollie and I were teenagers, we decided to take sewing lessons. I made a blouse; it was a very careless job, with crooked seams and poorly fitted sleeves. I pulled it on, knowing that I looked very sloppy but not really caring much until I saw Papa's face. "Corrie, the servant girl may be able to teach you how to scrub a floor, but your mother should teach you how to sew. When you spend your time and money on making something, it should be your best effort."

Achievement and honesty were such basic ingredients in Papa's personality that there were times when we had to hide the giggles he disliked so much. One of the stories Mama told about him was, "My husband is so honest that when the children were babies, he wouldn't allow me to give them a pacifier, no matter how loud or how long they cried. He would say, 'They think they are getting a drink. That is fooling a child to put something in her mouth which is a lie.'"

Mama would sigh with amused resignation and say, "So my babies never had a pacifier, because my husband is so honest."

Papa was honest about pain too. Whenever we had to go to a dentist or a doctor, Papa would come along to comfort us. However, he would never say that we would not have pain. He said that if we had to have a tooth filled or pulled that we must be brave and strong. Whenever it was possible, he went with us. Holding his hand gave us courage. If the doctor did need his assistance, his strong hands kept our hands or head from moving.

Perhaps it is wrong to tell this today—in view of the permissive way in which many children are being raised—but we were disciplined without spanking. I cannot remember being paddled as a child, but there was no doubt in our family that we were to obey Father. His will was law, and we all knew it.

We never spoke about the "line of authority" in our home—it was simply understood. Father didn't have to stand up and say, "I'm the head of this family!" He just was. We never felt any desire to have it any other way, because the love and security of all our relationships were built upon the established fact that God was always with us, and He had appointed Casper ten Boom in charge of the mansion in Haarlem called the Beje.

# 6

## Around the Oval Table

C an a piece of furniture be important? The oval table in our dining room was the gathering place for hopes and dreams, the listening place for prayers and petitions, and the loving place for joy and laughter.

But Sunday it was something more—it was the special place for family and friends.

Sunday was an important day for us; it was a day when everything—from the clothes we wore to the spoons we used—was distinctive. My Sunday dress was the new one I received for Christmas, so I seldom had a choice about what I would wear to church. Tante Anna could work magic with that dress, adding a colored sash or a ribbon in a way that improved my rather careless appearance. It was another of her small gifts of service that said, "I care."

When we were ready for church, Father would lead the way to St. Bavo's while we trailed along, trying not to scuff our shoes or muss our Sunday outfits.

After church it was good to go home, especially when the weather was chilly, for St. Bavo's was unheated, and there were days when my teeth would chatter through the entire service.

At home I would help with the Sunday dinner, first by smoothing a beautiful white cloth over the oval table. I tried to do this carefully, because I knew that Betsie wanted it to hang evenly, and it was a great desire of mine to meet her standards. Everything about Betsie was neat and I was . . . oh, well—just Corrie.

"Good work, Corrie," she would say, and that was all I needed to encourage me for the rest of the day.

The delicate china, which had been brought from Indonesia by father's older sister, Tante Toos, and Tante Jans's ornate silver service—a gift from wealthy members of her husband's church—were placed on the table. Then Tante Anna would emerge from the kitchen, wiping her hands on the generous apron she used to cover her black silk dress, and ring a little bell.

"Come to dinner, everyone."

When we were seated, Father would remove his fresh Sunday napkin from its holder, place it carefully on his lap, and bow his head.

"Lord, we thank You for this beautiful Lord's Day and for this family. Bless this food, bless our queen, and let soon come the day that Jesus, Your beloved Son, comes on the clouds of heaven. Amen."

Our table talk on Sunday sometimes centered around the sermon we had heard, but usually Father was cautious not to say too much. He attended the cathedral near our home because he felt that God had called him to that place, but he didn't hold any position in the church. His views were not accepted by the liberal thinkers who were in positions of leadership.

Conversations around the dinner table were lively because we all had stories or experiences we wanted to share. I believe that the great enjoyment of a family eating together is having this time when each person can be heard.

Father had a special talent in directing our talks so that no one would feel left out. We loved to tell personal stories but were taught to laugh at ourselves, not to make fun of others.

I remember one time when Nollie was telling about a painting she had done in school.

"I thought the drawing was rather good," Nollie said, "but when Mr. van Arkel walked over to my desk, he held up my picture and looked at it one way and then another, scowling all the time."

"Maybe he just wanted to get a better view," Betsie offered.

"I'm afraid that wasn't his reason," Nollie answered.

(Studies were important in our family, so each one of us received special attention when we talked about school.)

"What did Mr. van Arkel say, Nollie?" Mother asked.

"He said, 'Do you know of which Proverb your drawing reminds me, Nollie ten Boom?'"

"I told him '*Honi soit qui mal y pense.*' [Disgraced is he who thinks wrong of it.] It's from a motto on a badge of knighthood. Boy, did Mr. van Arkel laugh!"

Nollie's eyes twinkled when she told the story. Father really enjoyed a good joke, as long as the girls didn't giggle. Laughter he loved, but giggling was *verboden*.

On Sunday afternoons we frequently had visitors who would stop for a cup of tea and conversation. Sometimes we would go for a walk, but we didn't study, sew, or work on the Lord's Day. The only work allowed was winding the watches that were in the shop for repair.

Father said, "Even on Sunday, I must milk my cows."

## Father's Friends

Fellowship around the oval table was more than just a family affair. Throughout the years there were many people, young and old, rich and poor, who contributed so much to the richness of my childhood. I loved to have some of Father's friends visit in our home, because they laughed a lot and always told wonderful stories.

When Father was a young man in Amsterdam he worked in a mission called *Heil des Volks*, which was in a very poor part of the city. There were three other men who gave their time and energy to this particular outreach, and they all became fast friends.

The four men would meet often, sharing their burdens and triumphs, studying the Bible together, and discussing many topics of interest. As a child, I was always happy when they came to our house; it was a time when I loved to listen to the conversations of these great friends and learn from their experiences. The children were welcome to stay during their discussions and encouraged to participate if we had something we wanted to ask. I can still recall the fragrant mixture of cologne and good Dutch cigars that lingered in the room.

Frits Vermeer was a rather round Dutchman who loved to joke. He was "Uncle Frits" to us, just as the other good friends were called Uncle Dirk and Uncle Hendrik.

One of the first things Father would do when his friends arrived was to bring out the box of cigars from its place in the desk where the bulky ledger of the shop was kept. From his pocket, he would take the special cigar clipper that had keys for winding the clocks on the other side. It was a very important tool, and many children over a span of half a century sat on his lap and played with it.

Uncle Hendrik was considered the theologian of the group and was constantly being challenged for a Bible verse to meet some situation or problem. He was seldom at a loss when asked to quote something appropriate for the occasion.

Uncle Dirk, the fourth member of the group, was the only one who wasn't married. However, he loved children very much and was able to express that love in a special way.

On one occasion, when Father's friends were discussing their concerns, Uncle Dirk was anxious to tell about an orphanage where he was on the board of directors. I sat up and listened carefully, because children without parents bothered me so much. I thought how terrible it would be not to have the love of a mother and father.

"I decided to become the father of the orphanage," Uncle Dirk announced. "I have been on the board of directors, arguing for better conditions for those poor children, but I have not seen any positive results. I must get in there and work myself."

Father was delighted. "Dirk, this is certainly the leading of the Lord for you. He has not given you a wife, but He is going to bless you with many, many children. We will pray about it."

Father would begin to pray with his friends in an attitude that was so easy and natural that the conversation never seemed to stop; it would flow easily from friend to friend to the Lord.

Many times through the years I remember the wonderful moments I had listening to the stories and experiences of Father's friends. There is a Proverb that says, "Do not forsake your own friend or your father's friend" (Proverbs 27:10). I have often thought how wise that is.

## Bible Study Was a Game

With the dishes cleared off and kitchen duties accomplished, the oval table could be turned into a place for games. We didn't play cards (for that was considered a form of gambling), but we had a lasting enjoyment in the type of games that taught us something.

Different languages were introduced as a game, not as a forced study. When I was in the fourth grade, we began to learn French. As I remember, I loved the melodious sounds of this beautiful language, but it was and remained a difficult language for me. The next year I started English, which was easier, but I wondered as I struggled with all the different English meanings for words if I would ever go to England or America and have an opportunity to use the language.

Father wanted me to learn English well, and he gave me a little Sunday school booklet in English that was called "There's No Place Like Home." I read it over and over again.

The greatest fun in language learning came during our Bible study. The entire family would take part, each one of us having a Bible in a different language. Willem usually had the original in Hebrew and Greek; I would have the English; Mother the Dutch; Nollie the French; and Betsie or Father, German. It was a special and joyous time for us.

Father would begin by asking what John 3:16 was in English. I would answer from my English Bible, Mother from her Dutch Bible, and Betsie would reply in German.

When I was so young, it didn't seem possible that Betsie would ever have a chance to use a Bible verse in

German. We didn't know any Germans then! However, God uses such seemingly insignificant ways to prepare us for the plan He has for our lives. Over forty years later, in a concentration camp in Germany, Betsie was able to use that verse—and many more—to speak to the prisoners and the guards about God's love.

## When Father Prayed . . .

Every room in our house heard our prayers, but the oval table probably experienced more conversations with the Lord than other places. Praying was never an embarrassment for us, whether it was with the family together or when a stranger came in. Father prayed because he had a good Friend to talk over the problems of the day; he prayed because he had a direct connection with his Maker when he had a concern; he prayed because there was so much for which he wanted to thank God.

When Father talked with the Lord it was serious but unpretentious. He talked to Someone he knew. Once we had a minister in our house, and when his visit was over, Father prayed, "Thank you, Lord, for a good day. We hope everyone goes together in the same way."

The minister left with a puzzled expression on his face. Could this be the Casper ten Boom so many of his parishioners told him had such a deep understanding of God's Word?

Father always prayed before and after each meal. He included two things in his prayer: the queen and the second coming of Jesus Christ.

The knowledge and anticipation of the return of Jesus Christ was given to me by Father during one of the quiet, thoughtful times before I went to sleep as a small child. As for the queen—patriotism and loyalty were an accepted way of thinking in our house, as it was in most Dutch homes. However, I never thought that the prayers of the little ten Boom girl would be answered in such unusual ways.

## Me? A Guest of the Queen? Not Me!

It was the year 1956, more than half a century after I first heard Father pray for the queen. I was in Formosa with Dr. Bob Pierce, a man whose outreach of love and concern has spread throughout the world. He said to me one day, "Corrie, I believe it would be a good idea for you to talk with the queen of your country."

Bob is an American, and I forgave him for not understanding about proper protocol with members of royalty. *How ridiculous*, I thought.

"Bob, you don't know what you're saying . . . I can't go see the queen."

He looked at me gently and said, "Just pray about it." And so I did.

Wilhelmina had been queen through two world wars; her reign had spanned two generations, and now she had abdicated and given the position of monarchy to her only daughter, who is our Queen Juliana. Wilhelmina chose to have the title of *Princess* from that moment on.

When I was back in my homeland, I wrote to Princess Wilhelmina and said that I would like to meet her and bring greetings from Bob Pierce and World Vision International. The day after my letter was delivered, the princess sent her car to pick me up.

I sat in the back seat of the limousine, enjoying every kilometer from Haarlem to *Het Loo Apeldoorn*, where her palace was.

*Wouldn't Father have loved this*, I thought. *All those years he prayed for the queen and here is his daughter, Corrie, having a visit with Princess Wilhelmina herself!*

One amazing thing after another happened. I was given the opportunity of speaking with the queen and meeting all the people in the palace. After a few hours, I had to tell Princess Wilhelmina that I had to leave for some meetings that were planned in Germany.

She looked at me and said, "I expected you to stay several weeks here, and you're just staying a few hours. Why are you going to Germany?"

The war had been over for more than ten years, but its memories were still vivid to many Hollanders.

"I must go to Germany, your Highness, because God has called me to tell them of His love and forgiveness."

She dismissed what I was saying with a wave of her hand, but later when I returned once more to Holland she sent word for me to come and stay in the palace for a long time. I was allowed on that visit one hour each evening with Princess Wilhelmina. She said, "I'm too old for too much, so we may either eat together or talk for an hour." I chose the last part and had my meals with her lady-in-waiting afterward. Princess Wilhelmina knew her Bible very well, and we enjoyed those hours in her lovely private chamber. She gave me the opportunity to tell her of the miracle God had worked in my life to forgive my enemies.

I believe that in some way something of Father's prayers many, many years before were answered when

God allowed the daughter of the watchmaker to carry His message of love to the queen.

I had a happy time of fellowship with many people in the palace. I had personal contact with most of them when we talked about the most important person, our Lord Jesus Christ. But the happiest moments of each day were the hours with that great lady who had reigned over our little country in a time when two world wars had wounded Europe.

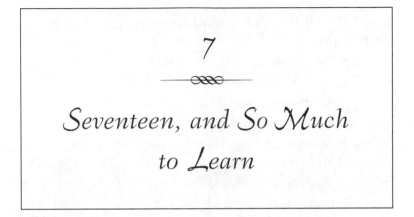

# 7

## Seventeen, and So Much to Learn

When Betsie told a story, she wove threads of brilliant color through the word pictures she created. When she moved into a room or dressed for a meeting, it was with a special flair. She knew *levenskunst* (the art of living)!

I wasn't what people would call a "mature" teenager. I was a tomboy during my adolescence—not a "young lady." However, I loved imitating and wanted to learn, but it didn't seem possible to me that I would ever have those soft qualities of womanhood that were so natural to my older sister.

Betsie taught me many things, and one of them was how to tell a story. She had a Sunday school class for many years, starting to teach when she was seventeen. She loved her pupils, and the little gifts and adoring glances she received from those boys and girls proved that her love was returned many times. One day she said to me, "Corrie, you must take a class too."

"What can I teach?" I asked, thinking how embarrassed I would be if someone asked me a question I couldn't answer. There was so much I didn't understand, especially all those kings and judges and battles in the Old Testament.

Betsie's answer was, "Try it! Tell the story of the feeding of the five thousand."

Now there was a story I knew! So I went with her to her class, believing this was a very simple assignment. What an embarrassment! How inadequate I felt when I finished the story in five minutes. The class was thirty minutes long, and I didn't know how to fill the remaining time. Betsie took over, and I listened with amazement as she told the same story over to a spellbound class of kids.

I was rather discouraged; I didn't know how to tell a story, but after that experience I was determined to learn. As I listened to Betsie I realized that you must weave a tale, leading your listeners on a word journey.

A girlfriend of mine, Mina, was a teacher in a Christian school, and she promised to help me. We asked permission of the director of the school to allow me to give the Bible story in her class every Monday morning. They were pretty drab at first, but gradually I began to learn how to add those imaginative touches that made them more interesting.

I used the technique of describing one picture after another, leading my little class through the art gallery of the Bible. When I told the story of the feeding of the five thousand again, we visualized Jesus with all the people sitting on the grass around Him. We would look at these people individually, imagining where they lived, what sort of problems they had, and what they might be thinking about this Man with the divine love in His eyes. The next picture is of Jesus and His followers, the disciples, talking about how the tired, hungry people were going to be fcd. There was no bakery or fish market within sight, but there was an obvious need for food. The blue waters of the Galilee reflected the surrounding green and brown hills, and the luxuriant grass where the people sat to listen to Jesus was pressed to the ground by the crowd.

Then I would carry my listeners with me to the climax, as Jesus took the five loaves and two fish offered Him by a boy who had gone shopping for his mother, and "looking up toward heaven, He blessed the food and broke the loaves and He kept giving them to the disciples to set before them; and He divided up the two fish among them all. And they all ate and were satisfied" (Mark 6:41–42).

"What a feast we have when we believe Jesus Christ!" I would end.

I had no idea how valuable this lesson was going to be in later life. If Betsie had told me that someday I would be speaking before thousands of people, I'm sure that the fear of such a thing would have silenced my clumsy efforts at storytelling immediately.

## From Bach with Love

Music was as much a part of my young life as television is to the children of today. Mother and Tante Anna had taught kindergarten, and I can remember them singing to me the little songs they taught to their schoolchildren. When I was old enough to sit at the organ called the harmonium and pump the pedals with my feet, Tante Jans had arranged for one of her military visitors to give Nollie and me music instruction.

We loved to sing in our house. Nollie had a rich

soprano voice, Willem sang tenor, and I was the alto when we learned to sing the Bach chorale "*Seid froh die Weil.*" I grew up loving Bach.

One time Father called us together and said, "We're going to St. Bavo's tomorrow evening for a great treat!"

I couldn't imagine anything that could be better than some of the concerts we had already enjoyed at Uncle Arnold's church. Because of Uncle Arnold's position as caretaker, we were given special permission to listen to the concerts, sitting on the bench beside the door that separated his home from the main sanctuary. Only the people who had money could afford to attend these fine concerts, and without Uncle Arnold, all the members of the ten Boom family would seldom have been able to enjoy such riches.

"Wear your warm clothes," Mama warned, as we were getting ready for the mysterious treat.

St. Bavo's was a vast, unheated building with foot-warmers for those who could afford to pay, and a hard wooden bench with cold stone at our backs for Uncle Arnold's relatives.

We all lined up, excited over the anticipation of Father's "great treat," and went to the cathedral, bypassing the front entrance and going in the side door to our own special reserved seats. The smell of moisture and dust, smoldering gas lamps, and the burning coals in the footwarmers was so familiar, and the excitement began to build. We sat down, with Father wrapping a wool blanket around Mother and placing a pillow at her back to make her more comfortable.

A wiry man with unruly gray hair and a drooping mustache passed us before going upstairs to the world-famous pipe organ. I had explored the area where this impressive organ stood and wondered how anyone could learn to play on so many manuals with sixty-eight stops. We had been told that Mozart played that organ when he was only ten years old.

We soon knew why the evening was going to be such a treat. I held my breath as Albert Schweitzer began playing a Bach prelude. He was an authority on organ building and an organist who could fill the cathedral with exquisite beauty. During the day St. Bavo's was a composition in gray, inside and out, but in the evening—with the gas lamps giving a Rembrandtesque light, the pillars pointing upward in a mysterious glow—the atmosphere of harmony was heaven. I thought eternity must contain this kind of beauty.

Albert Schweitzer was a German philosopher, physician, writer, and theologian. He had gone to Africa as a medical missionary and established a hospital and a leper colony. As his fame grew throughout the world, I often thought of the first time I heard him interpret Bach and how much Father's treat contributed to my lifetime love of music.

## Impatient to Learn Patience

We are not born with patience, and I believe God began to teach me something of what this means when I was in my seventeenth year. Because I was the youngest of the family, I remained childlike for a long time. I loved life intensely, charged with the desire to cram every available experience into each day. Then came a terrible blow that depressed me so severely I thought I wouldn't survive.

For some weeks I had a slight fever. For a time I managed to disguise how I felt, but soon Mama began to see my listless attitude and called the doctor. He probed and tapped, listened and questioned, and then told me I had tuberculosis.

Death sentence! *So young,* I thought . . . *why would God want me with Him when there was so much for me to do on earth?*

"You must go to bed, Corrie, until the fever is gone," the doctor pronounced.

In those days tuberculosis was as fearful as cancer is now. I cried and went upstairs slowly, not looking back. It was the middle of the day and it seemed strange to undress and go to bed!

I cried to the Lord, "Why must I be ill, Lord? I will live! I will be healthy!" It took many days before I could surrender and accept the situation. I surely had to learn what it says in Colossians:

> We pray that you will be strengthened from God's boundless resources, so that you will find yourselves able to pass through any experience and endure it with courage. You will even be able to thank God in the midst of pain and distress.
>
> 1:11–12 PHILLIPS

Through my tears and anger, I would thank Him, but I couldn't understand why He wanted me to lie in bed, imprisoned by the walls of my little room.

At first many visitors came upstairs, but after several months had passed, some people forgot me. I began to feel more self-pity and rebellion, but I prayed every day for peace in my heart, and finally the moment came when I could say, "Yes, Lord, you know best."

At that time Willem was a theological student at the

University of Leiden. He was going to have an examination in church history and often came home on weekends.

"I get things in my head if I teach them. How about
it, Corrie. If I give you some books, will you study them?"

It was not the first time I had to assist him in that way.
To earn some money in his college time, he gave lessons
in Latin to a boy who was a very unwilling pupil. Every
morning from seven until eight o'clock he taught him, and
I joined the two of them. If the boy didn't listen and was
absolutely uncooperative, then Willem taught me Latin. I
enjoyed those lessons and knew that my brother was a
good teacher.

I gained a great love for church history during those
months of confinement, and it took my thoughts away
from my illness.

The doctor did not visit me much; rest was the only
cure he knew, and he told the family not to allow me to
get out of bed until there was no sign of a fever. One day
he passed my room after visiting Tante Bep, who was very
old and feeble, and I called him.

"Doctor, I have a pain in my abdomen. It's right here,"
I said, pressing my fist on my right side.

He examined me and found an appendix infection,
which was probably the cause of my fever all that time. I
don't think anyone has ever been so happy with appen-
dicitis! After five months of confinement I left my bed,
had a minor operation, and returned to the wonderful
outside world.

## In the World, but Not of It

Until that time in my life the outside world was very
small. It consisted of the streets and alleys of Haarlem,

with only brief excursions with Father to Amsterdam, or an occasional visit to a neighboring village to visit friends.

I began to want to be somebody outside the protection of the Beje—to learn about the world that existed away from the Barteljoristraat. I didn't dream that I could see some of the countries and people that I read about in my geography book, but at least I wanted to experience life outside the shop.

Was I wrong? I struggled with this ambition and decided to ask my Bible teacher, Mrs. van Lennep, who was a very understanding woman who counseled well. She said, "Corrie, it's very natural for you to feel the way you do. You can do something in the world through the power of the Lord."

The first thing I did was launch into an intensive study of many subjects. I received diplomas in home economics, child care, needlepoint, and others. It proved to be a good background for my first job.

My opportunity came to be "out in the world." I heard about a job from one of the girls at school. The Bruins, who had a magnificent home, needed an *au paire* for their little girl. This position was a combination governess and companion. I knew this was what Tante Bep had done in her youth—and she had become a lonely and rather dour old woman—but this didn't quench my original enthusiasm for what I thought would be a new adventure in living.

Father and Mother gave their permission, and I packed my few clothes in a little suitcase and left with great anticipation for Zandvoort, a village by the sea, about ten miles from Haarlem.

The contrast between my homelife and my new job

began with my first glimpse of the home. It was so big! How could just one family live in a house that size?

As I began my job, I tried very hard to please the entire family. At home I had always known fun and laughter, with a large dose of love and affection. Out in the world it wasn't the same. For the first time I was faced with a new way of thinking, a different kind of family life than I had ever experienced.

If this was the way to "be somebody," I wasn't sure it was what I wanted.

Thursday was my day off, and it was such a relief to go back to Haarlem for my catechism lessons. Going home each week only made me realize the contrast between the security of our family and life in the outside world. In some ways, it was disillusioning to me.

I had determined to do my very best as an *au paire*. I wanted to leave often, but I was not a quitter, so I stayed.

One day, however, Willem came to Zandvoort with the news that our oldest aunt, Tante Bep, had died. She had been an invalid in our house for many years, and Tante Anna had the full responsibility of nursing her after I left. Now Willem told me that Tante Anna was very tired and should have a long rest.

I told my employer that I must leave at once because I was needed at home. Freedom at last! In my heart I wanted to rejoice that I was going home, but under the circumstances it really didn't seem the proper thing to do.

As Willem took my little bag and we walked away from that house of luxury, I felt no regret. Willem said, "Let's go down to the beach—it's such a glorious day!" And then he began to sing Bach music very loudly.

Somehow I felt it was all right to rejoice inside, but I

didn't think it was right to let it show. "Willem, how can you do such a thing? Tante Bep has died and you shouldn't be acting so happy."

"Of course we would be happy, Corrie. A child of God is a citizen of heaven and the attitude of a Christian must be one of praise when someone has died. Our grief for Tante Bep would just be one of selfishness on our part, of grieving for the sake of ourselves."

I knew he was right, and when we arrived at the Beje, it was with our hearts at peace with the knowledge of the glory of Tante Bep's new home in heaven. How good it was to be home! There was a harmony there that was such a contrast with the rich home of my former employer. I realized then why Tante Bep had the type of personality she had. Just a small taste of the life she had led gave me more understanding. We never know until we walk in someone else's shoes.

## The Everlasting Arms

There were so many times when the problems of the moment, whether they were small or large, would overwhelm me. I remember at a time, not long after Tante Bep's death, when Mother became very ill. I was so worried about her, and in addition I knew there was a large bill that had to be paid within the next few days. People were not interested in buying watches at that time, and Father and I were sitting in the dining room talking things over.

I stared at the familiar red and black tablecloth that had seen happy and sad times. I felt so depressed. Everything was wrong, and there didn't seem to be any good thing that could come out of such a discouraging situation.

"Father, what must we do? Everything is so terrible!"

"Don't forget, Corrie—underneath us are the ever-lasting arms. We won't fall."

I didn't know that expression and I asked, "Is that in the Bible?"

"It certainly is. Moses spoke those words to the sons of Israel."

"How does that help us right now?" I asked rebelliously.

"Girl, it makes all the difference. Moses tells us in the Book of Deuteronomy that God is a dwelling place. We have the promise of security when His arms are beneath us . . . holding us . . . supporting us . . . strengthening us."

Thirty years later I was lying on a dirty mattress in a concentration camp. It was pitch-dark, and in that rest-less room Betsie lay so close to me that I could feel her heartbeat. It was irregular and feeble.

I tried to think of something comforting to say to her before we fell asleep, and suddenly I remembered the dining room, the red and black tablecloth, and Father saying in his calm voice, ". . . underneath are the ever-lasting arms."

"Betsie . . . are you asleep?"

"No, not yet," she said weakly.

"Remember what Father told us: 'God is our dwelling place. Underneath are the everlasting arms.'"

I can't be sure, but I believe she must have smiled in that black barracks.

"Oh, yes, Corrie . . . and they will never leave us."

# 8

## The Best Is Yet to Be

O ur concerns reached beyond the borders of Holland. We all wanted to know more about other lands, different languages, and people from contrasting cultures. This interest was stimulated by visitors from many countries, and by reading good books.

During my late teen years a man came to Holland who focused our attention on foreign missions. His name was Jan Willem Gunning, and he started a movement for "mission study advice." Betsie, Nollie, Willem, and I became involved in groups that he formed. During the summer we went to a conference in Lunteren, a center in the midst of the woods and heather fields. It was so exciting to meet real missionaries from all over the world.

On the first day of meetings, an elderly missionary led the hundreds of people at the conference in group singing, and our own Nollie was chosen to be a soloist.

"Nollie, isn't it thrilling? Imagine—you're going to sing for all those people," I said.

"Oh, Corrie, don't remind me or I won't be able to utter a sound."

It was a new experience for all of us. We listened to the lectures and then divided into smaller discussion groups. We chose what we wanted to study and later used the material in weekly meetings at home. Mission students from a large school led these discussions, and we became great friends with some of them.

Many girls we knew were interested in more than the study groups; the mission students were as new and different as the subjects we were being taught. Unfortunately, there was very little time for dates. In fact, the only time available was two hours before breakfast. I've never been very alert at an early hour, but I learned to accept the challenge of this discipline for the advantages of the friendships.

I slept with a little rope around my toe. When a boy came to meet me when I was still asleep, he pulled the end of the rope, which hung outside my window, and I would jerk to attention. Soon we would be walking together over the heather fields of Lunteren, talking about mission activities and what we wanted to do with our lives. It was innocent enough—but not the part of the conference I would relate to Tante Jans!

One boy, Albert de Neef, had a girlfriend who was not very strong. She had gone to her doctor for a physical to find out if she was healthy enough to go to Indonesia, but during the conference she heard that she had been rejected. Those two were very sad, so we invited her to come to the Beje for a visit. She had so much fun with us that she almost forgot her disappointment. However, a year later, during another mission study conference, she was reexamined and was given approval to go to the mission field.

Because of that little act of hospitality, we became quite popular among the mission students. A new world opened for all four of us when we started a mission study group at home.

We had such good training at those camps. I never dreamed how much this would mean years later when I became a tramp for the Lord and visited mission fields on five continents.

## Beyond the Dikes

My horizons began to stretch. At the camps for missions we met people from all over the world. Then through the YMCA in Haarlem we had further opportunities to know people from other countries and other denominations. The Y was only a building where young men could have meetings, but tourists came from other countries, expecting it to be a hotel. The manager didn't speak English, and many times he brought guests to the Beje, where he knew they would be welcomed. We could exercise our English, broadening our interest in the whole world situation at the same time.

I learned more about Christians who did not have the exact beliefs in some doctrines that we did. As a little girl, I had always thought that the Dutch Reformed Church was the only one that had the right theology. Others could love the Lord, I granted, but they really had a lot to learn!

As my interest in a true ecumenical faith grew, I began to learn about Christians who endured so much for their beliefs. Father once told me of Christians in Russia who were called Stundists. They loved the Lord and were willing to suffer for Jesus. They knew the Bible from cover to cover and were very strict in their behavior.

Father said, "God has given Russia a great blessing by sending these Christians to that country. They live in the vast area of Siberia in a kind of community life where young and old are trained to glorify the Lord."

It seemed so remote to hear about suffering of Christians. We were free in Holland, and it was difficult for me to imagine Christians in another land undergoing persecution.

More than half a century passed after Father told me about the Stundists. Ellen de Kroon, my secretary and companion, and I went to Russia. We traveled all the way to Tadzhik, far inside Russia near to Siberia, and there we found a lively church, so dedicated to the Lord that it was a light in that dreary land. These people were Stundists, and I remembered Father's story.

A very old woman, stooped with age, a lifetime of extreme hardships written on her face, came to me and said, "Corrie ten Boom, I have prayed daily for you for years."

I was astonished. "How did you know about me?"

"Once I got a care package from Germany. One of the boxes was packed with a page from a Christian magazine, and I read about your experiences and the work you do now. God told me to pray faithfully for you."

It never ceases to amaze me the way the Lord creates a bond among believers that reaches across continents, beyond race and color. This spiritual bond is something man has tried to establish with big national or world councils and organized ecumenical movements but always misses when the Spirit of the Lord is not present.

## Sadhu Sundar Singh

A person who influenced my life in my late teens was a man from India. As a boy he was taught to hate Jesus. He knew about God, but the Bible of the Christians was a book that he believed was a gigantic lie. Once he took a

Bible and burned it, feeling that with this act he could publicly declare his scorn of what he believed were the untruths it contained. When missionaries passed him he threw mud on them.

But there was a terrible unrest inside of him; he longed to know God. He told this story about himself:

"Although I had believed that I had done a very good deed by burning the Bible, I felt unhappy. After three days, I couldn't bear it any longer. I rose early in the morning and prayed that if God really existed, He would reveal himself to me. I wanted to know if there was an existence after death, if there was a heaven. The only way I could know it for sure was to die. So I decided to die.

"I planned to throw myself in front of the train that passed by our house. Then suddenly something unusual happened. The room was filled with a beautiful glow and I saw a man. I thought it might be Buddha, or some other holy man. Then I heard a voice.

"'How long will you deny Me? I died for you; I have given My life for you.'

"Then I saw His hands—the pierced hands of Jesus Christ. This was the Christ I had imagined as a great man who once lived in Palestine, but who died and disappeared. And yet He now stood before me . . . alive! I saw His face looking at me with love.

"Three days before, I had burned the Bible, and yet He was not angry. I was suddenly changed . . . I saw Him as Christ, the living One, the Savior of the world. I fell on my knees and knew a wonderful peace, which I had never found anywhere before. That was the happiness I had been seeking for such a long time."

When I first heard about Sadhu Singh, the stories seemed to grow, until it was impossible to separate fact from fiction. Then he came to Holland and was asked by some people who were active in mission work to come to a weekend conference at Lunteren. I was so excited about the possibility of hearing him that I went to the conference grounds, although I knew it was booked to capacity.

With a rucksack and a blanket under my arm, I arrived at the entrance to the camp house. A tall student by the name of van Hoogstraten was giving out cards for the rooms. When he came to me I said, "I don't have a reservation, but I can sleep out in the field. I would just like to attend the meetings with the Sadhu."

The student smiled at my determination and said, "Miss ten Boom, there's a room for you. You're welcome here."

This same young student later became a missionary and died in a Japanese prison camp during World War II. The kindness he showed me was one of his characteristics, and years later he was a blessing to his prison guards. One of his daughters, Connie, later became my first companion for seven years as I toured the world.

That weekend, as I listened to the Sadhu, I was amazed but disturbed. He told of the visions he had seen—of how he really saw Jesus—at a time when he didn't believe. We had all read about the apostle Paul's experiences on the road to Damascus, but here was a man who claimed to have had this experience himself.

One boy ventured to ask the question we all wanted to know. "Please, sir, how did Jesus look?"

He put his hand before his eyes and said, "Oh, His eyes, His eyes . . . they are so beautiful." Since then I have longed to see Jesus' eyes.

Nobody moved or spoke. The Sadhu's face was the

most Christlike face I've ever seen. It made me happy and sad at the same time.

After the meeting I needed to think, and so I started to walk through the heather by myself, trying to understand all I had heard, questioning my own relationship with God.

As I was walking, I was deep in my own thoughts and almost ran into the Sadhu, who was going for a stroll too. I worked up my courage to ask him some questions but soon found he was very easy to talk to. He put me completely at ease.

"Please, Mr. Sadhu, tell me what is wrong with me? I'm a child of God, I have received Jesus as my Savior, and I know that my sins are forgiven. I know He is with me for He has said, 'I am with you always 'til the end of the world.' But what's wrong with me? I've never seen a vision or experienced a miracle."

The Sadhu smiled at me. "Sometimes people come to me to see a miracle. When they come now I'll send them to Corrie ten Boom. That I know Jesus is alive and with me is no miracle . . . these eyes have seen Him. But you, who have never seen Him, know His presence. Isn't that a miracle of the Holy Spirit? Look in your Bible at what Jesus said to Thomas in John 20:29: 'Blessed are they who did not see, and yet believed.'

"Don't pray for visions; He gives you the assurance of His presence without visions."

It was such a relief to me . . . it seemed as if the Lord had thrown a curtain aside and I could see the light. Yes, it's a tremendous thing that we can know the Lord is with us!

Paul has said, "I know in whom I have believed."

And Peter . . . how beautifully he expressed it:

And though you have never seen Him, yet I know that you love Him. At present you trust Him without being able to see Him, and even now He brings you a joy that words cannot express and which has in it a hint of the glories of Heaven; and all the time you are receiving the result of your faith in Him—the salvation of your own souls.

*1 Peter* 1:8–9 PHILLIPS

## Sharing

When I went home after that conference I couldn't wait to tell what I had experienced. It was early in the morning and Tante Anna was still in bed. I woke her up and began to spill out what had happened. I couldn't stop talking.

Betsie and the others heard me and came in, all of us crowding on the bed. I tried to recall everything I had heard and finally, when I paused long enough for anyone to comment, Tante Anna said, "It's just as if you have seen and heard one of the disciples of Jesus."

Father said, "Isn't it wonderful to have such joy here on earth? It's a little foretaste of heaven. Yes, the best is yet to be."

Father often said that after we had shared some particularly rich occurrence.

Years later when Father entered a door of a prison, he said, "Remember, Corrie, the best is yet to be." After ten days Father's spirit stepped out of that prison and into paradise.

The best had arrived.

# 9

---
∞∞∞
---

# Love and a Sound Mind

It was 1909. The world around us was bursting with change; an American explorer, Robert Peary, had reached the North Pole; the doomed *Lusitania*, one of the largest and most modern ocean liners, was steaming luxuriously across the Atlantic; in Russia the tsar was beginning a program of persecution against the Jews, while in Palestine a young man, David Ben Gurion, was dreaming of a return of God's chosen people to their ancient land.

The early part of the twentieth century was preparing the way for a surge of science and an upheaval of society. In Holland, however, our attention was upon the birth of a baby princess, Juliana, heiress to the throne.

In man's never-ending quest for man-made peace, the leaders of the world were gathering in The Hague, Holland, to make another attempt to form an international body, where nations might try to solve their disputes.

Nollie, Willem, Betsie, and I were young people intensely involved in our own pursuits and yet revolving around each other.

Nollie was a naturally gifted teacher; eventually it became her profession. At one time she taught in Haarlem under a headmaster who was a very narrow-minded, disagreeable man. It was so painful to see our sweet, fun-loving Nollie become depressed on Sunday evening as she thought of the next day, when she would have to face her school superior again. Her face would get longer and longer, but she knew the children loved her so she continued as a first-grade teacher.

Eventually she went to another school in Amsterdam, and this took her away from home for the first time. She met Flip van Woerden, also a teacher, and they were married. The Lord gave her seven children, and she had a better chance to use her motherly gifts than in the classes at school.

My dear, studious brother, Willem, with his precise beard and inquiring mind, provided an intellectual stimulus to our conversations and home life. Although Willem was the natural heir to Father's business, he did not have the inclination toward watchmaking, preferring to study theology instead. Father never pushed his children into work that they didn't want, and consequently, Willem did not feel that he was disappointing Father by not following in his footsteps.

We all loved music, but Willem had only one favorite composer—Bach. We learned to sing Bach chorales just as most children learn nursery songs. Nollie sang soprano, Willem, bass, and I, alto. How fortunate we were to have a brother, because Bach with a ladies' trio would have been rather frothy!

Willem did not have any girlfriends, so when he told his friends at the university that he had asked Tine to marry him, Karel, his good friend, said, "I never thought you would marry! You never looked at any girl."

When he had been married ten years Willem was called to be a minister for the Jews. He went to Dresden,

Germany, and studied in the Delitcheanum. His thesis was written on racial anti-Semitism, a subject that may not have pleased some of his professors. He wrote that the severest pogrom in the entire history of the world could come in Germany. The amazing fact is that this study was presented by Willem in the year 1930, three years before the birth of Hitler's Third Reich.

I admired my brother very much and sometimes wondered why God hadn't made me an intellectual. Perhaps he could use my simple way of thinking in some way, I thought—but I certainly didn't know how!

When I looked at Betsie, it was usually accompanied by a sigh. Betsie had beautiful curls, my hair was straight. Betsie was neat and lovely, I was put together as an afterthought. How I loved Betsie, who was seven years older than I. She was not able to work hard, because she was weakened by severe anemia, but she managed to accomplish so much.

Betsie could turn a drab room into a place of charm; she could transform a dull happening into a rollicking, amusing story. We were introduced to art at an early age, and Betsie could make an art exhibit a tremendous treat, when she was the guide.

We were so rich in art in Holland and very conscious of our heritage from the masters of the past. When Betsie took me to the Frans Hals museum in Haarlem, she would point out the beauty of each masterpiece.

"Look, Corrie, at the way Hals paints the faces of his subjects. Aren't they marvelous? And look at their hands—have you ever seen anything more beautiful?"

She would explain to me the exceptional talents of Rembrandt, showing me how he expressed the character of those he painted. Betsie could weave stories through a visit to an art exhibit in such an exciting way that I couldn't wait for the next chapter. It added to the richness of my childhood and the quality of my appreciation for classical art and music.

Betsie didn't promote herself; she remained in the background, always helping and ready with good advice and a sense of humor. Sometimes she assisted Father with his weekly paper, which he wrote for watchmakers, turning an ordinary report on a visit to a factory into an original, humorous story.

The church of our childhood and later years was the *Grote Kerk*, or St. Bavo's, the grand old cathedral that played such an important part in our lives. In the late afternoon there was a service called the "everyday church," which was supposed to last about half an hour. Usually not more than twenty persons attended, but the ministers were obligated to conduct the service for the faithful few. Since it is human nature to forget a job you do not like, sometimes the ministers did not appear.

When I was in my late teens and early twenties, my cousin, Uncle Arnold's son, took his father's job and was usher, or caretaker, of St. Bavo's. He often telephoned me and said, "Corrie, no pastor turned up for the service this afternoon. Please come and help us out."

I remember once when that request came I had a particularly full day at the house and in the shop, and my head was blank of any message I could bring to the small gathering of people. I ran to the kitchen where Betsie was cooking, hoping she would have a suggestion.

"Betsie, what in the world can I tell the people at the cathedral?"

Her answer came without hesitation; it was as if she had prepared it all day. While she told me the sermon, she brushed my coat, fixed my hair, and looked critically at my appearance.

"Keep your coat on, Corrie; your dress isn't too clean. Take Psalm 23 as your subject—'The Lord is my Shepherd.' Sheep can be very stupid, you know. Sometimes they don't see food behind their backs. We need the Lord just as much as sheep need a shepherd."

Betsie told me the whole outline of the sermon while she accompanied me to the door.

"I'll pray for you . . . I'm sure God will bless the message."

I was halfway through the little alley and turned to see her still standing in the doorway.

"Betsie, I can't think . . . what hymns should I give them to sing?"

"Just ask them for their favorites."

There was a blessing in the cathedral that day, while in the kitchen of our house, Betsie prayed.

She was tidy about her person, her possessions, and her thoughts. I remember years later I passed her cell in the German prison in Holland where we were political prisoners of the Nazi regime. The Red Cross had just sent a food package to the prisoners, and on the little corner shelf stood that food in neat rows. Over a stool was a handkerchief and a bottle with two tulips, a present from the judge with whom Betsie had prayed after the hearing. In those stark surroundings was an atmosphere of cleanliness and order, which was the stamp of Betsie's personality.

Although we had our individual interests, we loved a family project together. Mama and Papa's twenty-fifth anniversary was our chance to plan a real celebration. Nollie had been working as a teacher, and she had to supply the finances for the party. She had saved as much as she could in order to rent the hall of the YMCA. We planned the entertainment, but that was free—except for the personal price of courage I had to pay to perform before all the guests.

Willem came as Johann Sebastian Bach, playing his part with a dignified flourish. He was a musician, and I probably thought it was easy for him. Nollie, who loved to dress up, was Sarah Bernhardt. (Why hadn't I learned those social graces?)

The evening of the party Mother was flushed with excitement; I thought she had never looked more beautiful. Father es-corted her to the YMCA as if he were taking the queen herself to a royal ball. Dozens of friends from the rich to the servant class were at the party; merchants on the street; clients whose clocks Father repaired and wound; people to whom Mother had brought soup and comfort—all swarmed into the hall to bring their love and congratulations to the popular watchmaker and his wife.

When the party was almost over, I finally mustered the nerve to contribute my part to the entertainment. I was introduced with a flourish by Willem and stepped forward in a borrowed Salvation Army uniform. I can't remember whether the uniform fit or I sung on key, but I do know that an edge was taken off my shyness in my first public appearance.

The four of us had pooled our money to buy a silver serviette ring for Father and Mother, which Willem had engraved with a Hebrew inscription. It said: THE LORD IS GOOD. HIS MERCY IS FROM ETERNITY AND HIS FAITHFUL-NESS FROM GENERATION TO GENERATION.

The Lord was faithful in giving me the strength to sing in front of all those people. I don't think I dreamed when I was seventeen that I would be called to speak before thousands some day. His faithfulness is certainly "from generation to generation."

## Ethics, Dogmatics, and Bathtubs

In 1910, a Bible school opened in Haarlem. When I saw the program I was so excited. There was so much I wanted to learn. I plunged into this new enterprise, taking seven different subjects at one time. For two years I struggled with ethics, dogmatics, church history, Old Testament, New Testament, story of the Old Testament, and story of the New Testament. Such an undertaking might not be so difficult for a clever student—but that I wasn't.

During this time Mother suffered a slight stroke. Although she became weaker physically, her gentle spirit and positive attitude were an encouragement to all of us.

As my workload at home increased, it became more of a chore to keep up with my studies. Finally the day of judgment arrived—examinations. The first part was practical application; we had to give lessons and answer questions from students. I passed this quite well and was full of confidence when I appeared before the group of ministers who were to give me the second part of the examination.

The ministers gathered to interrogate me in a room that should have held no terror for me. It was a large conference room opening off a familiar corridor in St. Bavo's. Dot and I had played in that room as children, but when I saw the rather formidable-looking gentlemen sitting on both sides of the massive table, my courage began to wither. The fireplace on one side of the room was large enough for me to walk into, but I realized I was no longer a child hiding in the coatroom so the principal wouldn't see me.

The president of the church asked me the first question. "Miss ten Boom, what did you study for ethics?"

"I followed the teaching of Mr. Johnson for two years . . ." I began, but got no further.

St. Bavo's was usually chilly, but the icicles seemed to form on the ceiling. Pastor Williamson, the president, lifted his eyebrows and stared at me. He and Pastor Johnson had been theological students at the same university, and their disagreements were well known among the faculty.

"You studied nothing else?" Pastor Williamson asked disdainfully.

It was tense. I was tense. Suddenly I couldn't remember a thing. Out of seven different subjects I managed to get seven failing grades!

Willem, why didn't I have your brains?

When I returned home with the news of my defeat, Betsie was one of the first to console me. However, I didn't think she gave me the sympathy I deserved because she said, "You must do it again." Something about the way she said it made me repress my objections.

"When you have failed an examination, Corrie, you know your whole life that you have failed; when you do it again, then you know your whole life that you have succeeded and have the diploma."

Eight years later I took the examination again and passed.

The important lesson I learned from my Bible school experience was that from these organized studies we learn the wisdom of the wise but not much of the "foolishness of God."

The best learning I had came from teaching. I could serve the church by giving catechism lessons and preparing people who were to take their confirmation. In the Dutch Reformed Church you do this when you are eighteen years or older. I was also licensed to give Bible lessons in the non-Christian schools. Parents who sent their children to secular schools could elect to have their children take these lessons.

I learned to listen to the Holy Spirit when I prepared for the lessons, and when I talked with the children and young people, my "lessons" were more of a conversation with them than telling what I knew. It was a joy to learn in this way much of the reality of the gospel. Talking over my experiences with Father and the others was an added training. Besides this important result of that fruitful time, there was the new experience that I received a small amount of money for this and decided to save that special income for a very special project.


When I was growing up there was one luxury I wanted: a flush toilet. Of course we had toilets, one upstairs and one downstairs, but they were the accommodations that necessitated a once-a-month service from the workers in the city sanitation department. As I saved my small salary from the Bible teaching, it was with great anticipation of supplying the Beje with two porcelain pleasures.

Next—a luxury of pure ecstasy—I saved to buy a bathtub! Each room in the house had a bowl to use for washing, but we were very frugal with precious heat during the winter, and there were many mornings when we broke the ice to splash our faces.

When my "bathtub fund" was large enough to buy the splendid fixture, it was a thrilling day at the Beje. The bathtub was equipped with a gas water-heater so that it no longer was necessary to be polar bears to get clean. We had a platform built under the tub so the water would drain out.

Somehow all of those hours struggling over ethics, dogmatics, and all the rest of the subjects that enabled me to teach were worth it to achieve such a magnificent ma-terial goal. How I enjoyed that tub!

## Patriotism and Prayer

Discussing the truths of the Bible was as natural to our family as talking about sports or current events. It was remarkable how Father found so many contrasting people for his Bible study groups. It was this willingness to share his time with others that made him so rich with friends.

For three years we had a prayer meeting every Saturday night in Heemstede, a neighboring village. Father, Betsie, and I went on the streetcar to the meeting, in hot weather and cold, rain or snow; it was a regular part of our life.

In 1914, war swirled around our little country. Each nation had been trying to increase its own wealth and power for decades, and the threat of a clash was becoming a reality. Only five years had passed since The Hague Peace Conference, and yet all the great powers seemed to believe that threats and force were the tactics to use to get what they wanted. The world was en-gulfed in a terrifying game of fear.

From the time the Austrian crown prince, Archduke

Francis Ferdinand, and his wife were assassinated, one after another of the countries of the world issued declarations of war.

Father continued to pray for the queen and the government of Holland, as he always had. We were very patriotic and loyal to Queen Wilhelmina and her prime minister, Abraham Kuyper, who was also a prominent theologian.

A division of purpose developed in our weekly prayer group. "Casper, it's not right to pray for those in government," some of the people said. "The world is evil—Satan is prince of this world and we should only look at the kingdom of God."

But Father said, "As Christians we are in the world, but not of the world. We must not give over our country to the enemy, because then we would be disobeying 1 Timothy 2, which says, 'First of all, then, I urge that entreaties and prayers, petitions and thanksgivings, be made on behalf of all men, for kings and all who are in authority, in order that we may lead a tranquil and quiet life in all godliness and dignity'" (vv. 1–2).

As the weeks and months of World War I went on, the pietists became more uncomfortable as Father, Betsie, and I continued to pray for our government. The difference in these basic beliefs drove the group apart. The others began to draw more and more into their spiritual shells, until we could no longer meet together for prayer.

## Beyond This World

Father was not quarrelsome about his biblical beliefs, but he stood fast in theological debates, especially with Tante

Jans. They used to have some rather lively discussions, which Mother and I didn't enjoy.

Father was a Calvinist, and I heard him speak frequently about predestination. I never quite understood what he meant, so one time I asked, "What is predestination?"

He answered, "The ground on which I build my faith is not in me, but in the faithfulness of God."

That was an answer I enjoyed, and I repeated it many times in the years to follow.

One of the main points of dissension between Father and Tante Jans came over faith and works. In the Book of Philippians it is written: "So then, my beloved, just as you have always obeyed, not as in my presence only, but now much more in my absence, work out your salvation with fear and trembling; for it is God who is at work in you, both to will and to work for His good pleasure" (2:12–13).

Father talked more about "it is God who is at work in you . . ." and Tante Jans emphasized "work out your salvation." I believe the fear she had of death may have been the result of never quite believing she had worked hard enough for God.

## The Great Journey

One of the great human mysteries I shared with Father was why Tante Jans, a powerful evangelist, a woman with a zeal to teach and write about the Lord Jesus, had such a dread of dying. When the time came when we knew she didn't have much longer on earth, we didn't know how she would react.

Father loved Tante Jans, as we all did, in spite of her crusty manner and argumentative personality.

"Jans," Father patted her wrinkled hand gently, smiling into the no-longer stern face, "are you ready to make the great journey? The doctor has said that it can't be too long before you have to leave us."

Tante Jans's face lit up. "Jesus said, 'I give my sheep everlasting life.' That's good . . . I can't do anything more . . . I'm safe in the hands of the Good Shepherd who gave His life for us. He prepared a mansion in the house of the Father for me."

When the hour of death arrived, God took away her fear.

On the day of her burial the house was full of people who told how she had been used by the Lord to bring them to Him. We told them about the joy she had and that the fear of death had vanished the moment she knew she had to die. A friend of hers, a nurse, said, "I'm so glad to hear that. I often wonder if in the hour of death the devil will take away my assurance of salvation. I've seen so many Christian people die in agony, attacked by fear, although I knew they were children of God."

Another nurse, who had also come to honor her friend, gave some good advice. "Just tell the Lord that you have this fear . . . then pray that when the hour of death comes for you, Jesus will protect you against any attack of the enemy and that He will give you a clear experience of His presence. He said, 'I am with you always 'til the end of the world.' This prayer will be answered. I've seen many people dying too. All who prayed this prayer beforehand died in great peace and assurance of Jesus' presence and salvation. I could see it on their faces."

When the second aunt in our family died, it made me think more about time and eternity. We are citizens of heaven—our outlook goes beyond this world. I know the truth of the Bible, when it says that God doesn't give us a spirit of fear, but of power, of love and a sound mind.

## Her Silent Love

One morning I was talking to Father about a chance to make some attractive magazine advertisements for our business, when I heard the sound of a crash. I ran into the kitchen and saw Mother slumped by the sink; a large kettle had fallen on the floor. Her left arm hung limply at her side as she struggled to hold on to the counter.

"Mama, sit down, dear." I helped her to a chair and ran to get Father.

"Hurry . . . something's wrong with Mother."

Father rushed in and put his arms around her. She looked up and whispered in a voice that was barely audible, "Oh, Cas, we've been so happy together."

She thought she was going to die right then. We supported her carefully and guided her to her room. When the doctor had examined her, he comforted us by saying that strokes could be dangerous but frequently were not so serious. "One of my patients had a stroke and after that went to Switzerland three times. Your mother can live another eight or ten years."

Mother never fully recovered the use of her body after her next stroke, and for the remainder of her earthly life, her speech was limited to one word: "Corrie." With a word, the nod of her head, the opening or closing of her eyes, we saw a display of love that enriched all of us.

We developed a method of communication in which we would try to guess her thoughts, and she would answer with a motion of her head.

It was such a joy to be with her—and my own attitude

improved during the three years God allowed Mother to be with us after her most severe stroke. I began to understand what the verse in Romans meant that says, "For I consider that the sufferings of this present time are not worthy to be compared with the glory that is to be revealed to us" (Romans 8:18).

God's glory shone through Mother.

# 10

## Reach Out

Europe was devastated at the end of World War I; there was danger of starvation in war-torn countries, and yet there was also a resurgence of hope in the world. "Make the world safe for democracy" was the slogan of the Allies. The humanitarian compassion of the United States and the victor nations in sending supplies and food prevented millions from going hungry.

In Holland, we were thankful that we were spared from the terrible conflict, but we wanted to reach out with help to those who weren't so fortunate. What could the ten Boom family do?

Germany was a wounded country; many of its children were undernourished and suffering from severe malnutrition. We began to think of ways to provide homes for these children in Holland, building them up with good food and care, before returning them to their own homes. Since Father knew many watchmakers, he discussed with me how we could organize an outreach for children of watchmakers in Germany.

Father was chairman of the international watchmakers, a position he had earned not only because of the respect others in the profession had for him, but also because he was willing to work and keep his promises.

After the war, he spent many hours contacting watch-makers all over Holland to ask them to take a German child into their homes for a time.

"Why don't you take one yourself, Father?" I asked.

But Father was more realistic. "Just wait, Corrie. Many have promised to take children but not everyone will be faithful. We cannot depend on everyone. There will be children for whom I have no home and we can take them."

When the day came for the children to arrive, Father, Betsie, and I went to the railway station to see that each child went with the proper family. What a scene it was. The children stood on one side, shy, wistful, frightened, and the adults waited expectantly to find out which ones were to be a part of their households. One by one names were called, and someone would step forward to welcome the poor little things. An attempt had been made to match children with families who had girls and boys of the same age. I had to struggle to hold back my tears. Our little Dutch children were so ruddy-cheeked and sturdy beside the pale, undernourished Germans.

Soon everyone was accounted for—well, almost everyone. I had been watching one little girl pushing herself into the corner of the waiting room, as if she hoped to become a part of the woodwork. As each name was called, she tried to make herself less noticeable.

"Father, look at that girl—don't you have anyone left on your list for her?"

"Let's see . . . no, I don't believe so. We shall take her home with us."

My mind began to buzz. She could go to Willem's former room. (He had been married in 1916 to Tine, our doctor's sister.) I must see about some clothes for her—and perhaps we still had some dolls left in the attic.

Then we saw another one. A bedraggled little boy was waiting dejectedly for someone to claim him. Father checked his records and found out that the mother had become ill in the house where he was supposed to go. So we took Willy too.

"Come along, my young friends," Father said. "You need a good meal and a warm bed."

He reached down and held out his hands to two skinny little children, one about ten and the other a year or two younger. What a sight they made. Four spindly legs raced to keep up with Father's stride as we returned home.

Willy was a street urchin from Berlin. The ten Boom home, modest as it was, must have appeared like a palace to him. When the children sat down to the table and Tante Anna brought them soup, they both picked up their bowls and began to slurp, the excess making rivulets down their dirty chins.

"Corrie, these two must have a bath," Betsie announced, although the need was obvious to anyone who could see or smell.

Willy only spoke German, but the word bath must have a universal meaning for little boys, because he looked first at Betsie and then at me. There was sheer panic in his eyes.

Father sensed immediately that Willy thought these two funny ladies were going to subject him to the indignity of washing.

"Come along, sir, I will show you the most magnificent invention of our time!"

I'm sure Willy didn't understand what he was saying, but the tone of his voice and the flourish with which he directed him to the bathroom must have assured him that there was a marvelous treat in store.

After we tucked the children between clean sheets, Betsie, Father, and I went to Mother's room to tell her about the additions to our household. She couldn't understand German, but in the following weeks it was such an inspiration to us to see how she managed to love and help those German children. She could quiet a quarrel with the shake of her head or ease a hurt with outstretched hands.

"Isn't it wonderful," Betsie said, "to have children in the house? And what a blessing it is to have Willy. Father has been so outnumbered by females."

The next challenge soon arrived in the person of Mrs. Treckmann and her two little girls. We had known her through our association with the YMCA, and when she wrote from Germany that she was in desperate need of help and that her children were suffering from malnutrition, we started to make up more beds at once.

Mrs. Treckmann was more undernourished than her girls, Ruth and Martha. Her face was gaunt and lined with the strain of hardship, which war writes on the bodies and spirits of human beings. *Oh, Lord*, I thought, *don't ever put us through that in Holland. I don't think I would have the personal strength to watch my own family suffer.*

For the weeks their mother was with us in the house, the two little girls were rather difficult to handle. Ruth would throw temper tantrums, which threatened not only the wood paneling on my bedroom door, as she kicked it uncontrollably, but also the peace of our house, which was always active—but not with voices of discord. Her mother responded to these outbursts with several solid slaps across her face, which added to Ruth's rebellion.

Through Mrs. Treckmann's actions, we came in contact with the German way of discipline. Slapping for the slightest reason produced rather negative results, for Ruth responded with more tantrums.

In some way, without words, Mother taught Mrs. Treckmann that sometimes a beating on the bottom side of the anatomy was healthy, but slapping was not wise.

Mrs. Treckmann finally returned to Germany, but we kept Ruth and Martha, along with Willy and Katy, for quite a while. The first time Ruth began her door-kicking, attention-getting tantrums, we ignored her as if she were nothing more than a little fly buzzing around our deaf ears.

No slapping was required. Ruth and Martha became two of the nicest little ladies we ever had.

It was many years later that I received a letter from Ruth. She wrote that she had read some of my books and remembered the time she was in our house. "What a naughty girl I was, and what love I experienced in your home!" she wrote. "My husband and I pray that we can pass on the love we have received to people who need it. The Lord is our strength. How good to know that."

It was twenty-eight years later and I was in Germany. Another World War had engulfed the nations, and by this time I knew from horrible firsthand experience what it was to see my family and thousands of others suffer, even more than those in the First World War.

After a meeting in West Berlin I saw a neatly dressed gentleman smiling at me. Something about him jogged my memory. Of course—the little street boy with his slang and naughty eyes!

"Tante Corrie, do you remember me? I'm Willy, who lived with your family many years ago."

There was a new light in his eyes, and I wasn't surprised when he told me what had happened to him.

"I had never heard anyone pray in a house before. I knew that people went into the big cathedrals and said prayers, but when I lived with the ten Booms I heard praying before and after meals, and other times during the day. Many years later I accepted the Lord Jesus as my Savior, but I believe it was because you had planted those seeds of love in that skinny, frightened boy who came out of the slums of Berlin."

## The Saddest Day

The children from Germany stayed for a while, building their bodies and healing their spirits, before returning to their homeland. Those were growing years for all of us, but weakening years for Mother. Three years after Mother's severe stroke—times in which her love and patience spoke louder than any sermon—her physical life slipped away from us. Father saw the woman he had loved for so many years, the wife who gave him such strength, leave for her home in heaven.

She had taught us so much. She never pushed Father toward greater success in his business; she sustained him with her encouragement, no matter what trials he had. When money was scarce, she stretched what we had; when we met defeats, she taught us to try again.

Father looked at the woman he loved so much, knowing that she was with Jesus and that she was free of pain for the first time in many years.

"This is the saddest day of my life," he said. "Thank you, Lord, for giving her to me."

Father's loss was acute, but he did not engulf himself in self-pity. He knew where Mother was and he also knew that the Lord's work had to go on in this world.

# 11

---⦿---

# In and Out
# of the Watchmaker's Shop

Five . . . six . . . seven . . . eight . . . the chiming clocks in the shop told me it was eight o'clock in the morning. What a wonderful way to start the day . . . with the graceful Frisian clock singing the hour, the sonorous grandfather clock vibrating its bass melody, and a dozen or more pendulums joining the chorus. I hummed a little tune under my breath as I poked the fire under the coffeepot and brought one slice of white bread and one of brown bread out for Father's breakfast. He would descend the narrow staircase in exactly ten minutes. You could regulate your watch by his arrival in the dining room each morning.

This was the day Father wound the clocks in the homes of his wealthy clients. His breakfast must be prompt, for he was as disciplined as the timepieces he treated.

8:10 A.M. "*Goede morgen*, Corrie. You have been busy already, I believe."

He looked at the sacks lined up against the cupboards and knew that I had been up preparing meals for the day; meat, vegetables, potatoes, and stewed fruit started cooking before breakfast. I would begin the food in boiling water and then remove it from the stove for a special long-cooking method. Each pot would be wrapped in sixteen newspaper pages and then enclosed in a towel, sealing in the heat. It was a very effective and efficient way to cook and store food.

After breakfast and prayers, Father would go to our astronomical clock and check his pocket watch. The clock was impressive, taller than Father, with an accuracy that demanded synchronization with the Naval Observatory clock in Amsterdam. Neither cold nor heat affected the astronomical clock.

"Mmm . . . two seconds fast," Father commented. He adjusted his own timepiece precisely in preparation for the work of the day.

His bicycle was dusted, his hat adjusted, and off he went, pedaling intensely down the narrow Haarlem streets until he reached the homes of his clients in the suburbs of the city. He was an aristocrat and a servant, a gentleman of dignity and a confidante of the most lowly. Class distinction was very strong in Holland, but to him every human being was someone of value.

As he whirred through the streets he waved to many townspeople, endangering the security of his hat in the wind. When he arrived at the first house, breathless but prompt, he would go to the back door, ring the bell, and greet the servant girl who answered his summons.

"Hannah, how delightful to see your shining face this morning," he would say with a manner as gallant as one approaching royalty.

"Oh, Mister ten Boom, I'm so happy to see you. I've been reading the Book of John—just as you told me—and I have so many questions."

"Good, Hannah. I shall come to the kitchen for coffee at eleven o'clock. Perhaps some of the other servants will want to have a little talk too."

Father made everyone feel important, and in a home where there were twelve or fourteen servants, a downstairs maid or cook's helper might not have too much feeling of self-worth. Many of them looked forward all week to the arrival of the watchmaker.

His clients were people of means, many of them in the import business or owners of sugarcane plantations in Indonesia. The mistress of one mansion asked him which dancing school he attended, in order to learn how to bow in such a courtly manner.

Dancing school! Imagine such a thing. Father answered, "I never learned to dance, nor did I attend such a school. My father taught me manners."

Formal training had not been a part of Father's background. He left school when he was fourteen years old to become Grandfather's helper in the workshop. He attended night school for a time, but his training was not of a highly intellectual level. He was self-taught, especially from theological books and magazines. Sometimes when Willem explained to his fellow students at the university Father's answer to a problem, he would be asked, "Where did your father study theology?"

Father's horizon was wide, and he talked with even his most outstanding customers with wisdom and insight. He was equally at home in the kitchen and in the beautiful sitting rooms. He understood all these people because of the love in his heart, received through the Holy Spirit. (See Romans 5:5.)

Among the customers whose clocks he had to wind was a distinguished pastor and philosopher, Dominee de

Sopper. Father often asked him probing questions. After some months, the Dominee offered to give a course in philosophy in our home; although Father's beliefs didn't agree with this scholar's liberal views, the disputes between them didn't spoil their warm friendship.

For several winters this pastor, who later became professor of philosophy at the University of Leiden, had a weekly study group in our house. There were agnostics, atheists, fundamentalists, and liberals in this group, all with a quest for knowledge and none able to escape Casper ten Boom's direct answers to complex problems. "The Bible says . . ." he would say when the arguments became involved.

Father had nothing against philosophy, for he believed in a philosophy of living based upon the Word of God. However, he would express his differences when others would base their beliefs in such men as Kant and Hegel. Kant, the eighteenth-century German philosopher, had introduced a way of thinking that influenced many in the intellectual community. He did not believe in absolute right and wrong, and questioned whether people could accept things that were beyond their five senses. This would rule out spiritual realities or biblical truths. Hegel pursued the philosophy of relative thinking, which led to the basic political and economic ideas of Karl Marx and Adolf Hitler.

Without formal educational training, Father could debate the most brilliant with the Book he knew so well. He baffled some, converted others, and had the honest respect of all in that unusual study group.

## Out of the Frying Pan

When Father returned home after making his clock-winding rounds, I was anxious to hear what had happened.

"What did Mrs. van der Vliet say today? Did you see Pastor de Sopper? What about the cook at the de Boks'— has she been reading the Bible we sent?"

"Oh, Corrie, Corrie," Father laughed, "let's wait until after supper. The thought of the food you prepared this morning sustained me for the last five miles."

My job for many years was to assist Tante Anna in the housekeeping, cooking, cleaning, and nursing. Betsie worked with father in the shop as a bookkeeper, and I pursued the household tasks. I loved housekeeping; I found it challenging and creative. For instance, I tried to beat my own time records in washing and ironing. On Monday my goal was to have the clothes folded and put away by four o'clock. If I could make it by 3:30 or 3:45, I would reward myself with an extra fifteen minutes to half an hour of reading. I learned to bake bread, churn butter, and stretch a little to make a lot.

The division of labor at the ten Booms was suddenly changed by a flu epidemic in Holland. All the members of the family became ill. When Betsie was sick, I had to do her work in the shop; this was something I had never done before. I felt as if I had two left hands. It was a different world: meeting people, remembering their particular likes and dislikes, seeing in facts and figures the precarious balance of the family business.

When Betsie was well again, I made a suggestion. "Why don't we exchange jobs for a few months, so I can learn more about shopkeeping? I'm so terribly ignorant of what goes on in the business."

And so we switched. It was 1920; Willem and Tine had their own family, Nollie and Flip had been married a year, and the little German children had returned home. Time for a change.

I loved the work in the shop. The only thing I thought unpractical was that when a customer brought in a broken watch, I always had to ask Father, or one of our watchmakers in the workshop, to look at what repairs were needed or broken parts replaced.

"Father, I believe it would be useful if I learned watch repairing—will you teach me the trade of watchmaking?"

Immediately Father agreed. He had a great trust in my abilities.

"Of course I can teach you—and after some time I will send you to Switzerland to work as an apprentice in a factory. I hope you will become a better watchmaker than I am."

Dear Father, he was one of the best watchmakers in all of Holland; he wrote a book about the exact regulation of watches; he edited a weekly watchmaker's paper; he had been a pupil of Howu, one of the world's best clockmakers in his time. How could Father expect me to become better than he?

Tante Anna overheard his remarks and said, "Cas, I must warn you—Corrie will never give her full time to her trade. She always tries to do six things at a time."

Tante Anna was right. She was a woman with singleness of purpose: the comfort of our family. It must have been difficult for her to cope with the many directions of my attention, those ambitions of my heart that ignored the circumstances of our lives. I knew I was the youngest child of a respected businessman who did not have much money, and I was happy and content as such a person. But I believed there was more for me to do.

"Dear Lord," I would pray in the privacy of my little room, "can You use me in some way?"

## Blessed Money and Cursed Money

It took only a week for Betsie and me to know that changing jobs was right for both of us. Betsie, with her natural flair for beauty and order, added a new spark to the household. Cupboards were rearranged more efficiently, flowers appeared on the table and in windowboxes; even the meals seemed to have more imagination.

I loved the store and workshop. It had a very special atmosphere, and gradually I began to overcome my shyness and insecurity in meeting people, and enjoyed selling the watches and clocks. There were many ups and downs in the watchmaking business, but Father seemed to have a keen understanding of the economic situation of our times. In his weekly paper, *Christiaan Huygens*, he wrote information and suggestions for others in the business. Since he read all other papers about his trade in German, English, and French, he could adequately fill his paper with important news about trade and business.

However, when it came to making money in his own shop, it wasn't always so simple. He loved his work, but he was not a money-maker.

Once we were faced with a real financial crisis. A large bill had to be paid, and there simply wasn't enough money. One day a very well-dressed gentleman came into the shop and was looking at some very expensive watches. I stayed in the workshop and prayed, with one ear tuned to the conversation in the front room.

"Mmm . . . this is a fine watch, Mr. ten Boom," the customer said, turning a very costly timepiece over in his hands. "This is just what I've been looking for."

I held my breath as I saw the affluent customer reach into his inner pocket and pull out a thick wad of bills. Praise the Lord—cash! (I saw myself paying the overdue bill and being relieved of the burden I had been carrying for the past few weeks.)

The blessed customer looked at the watch admiringly and commented, "I had a good watchmaker here in Haarlem . . . his name was van Houten. Perhaps you knew him."

Father nodded his head. He knew almost everyone in Haarlem, especially colleagues.

"Van Houten died and his son took over the business. However, I bought a watch from him that didn't run at all. I sent it back three times, but it was just a lemon. That's why I decided to find another watchmaker."

"Will you show me that watch, please?" Father said.

The man took a large watch out of his vest and gave it to Father.

"Now, let me see," Father said, opening the back of the watch. He adjusted something and turned it back to the customer. "There, that was a very little mistake. It will be fine now. Sir, I trust the young watchmaker . . . he is just as good as his father. I think you can encourage him by buying the new watch from him."

"But, ten Boom!" the customer objected.

"This young man has had a difficult time in the trade

without his father. If you have a problem with one of his watches, come to me, I'll help you out. Now, I shall give you back your money and you return my watch."

I was horrified. I saw Father take back the watch and give the money to the customer. Then he opened the door for him and bowed deeply in his old-fashioned way.

My heart was where my feet should be as I emerged from the shelter of the workshop.

"Papa! How could you?"

I was so shocked by the enormity of what I had seen and heard that I reverted to a childhood term.

"Corrie, you know that I brought the gospel at the burial of Mr. van Houten."

Of course I remembered. It was Father's job to speak at the burials of the watchmakers in Haarlem. He was greatly loved by his colleagues and was also a very good speaker; he always used the occasion to talk about the Lord Jesus.

Father often said that people were touched by eternity when they have seen someone dying. That is an opportunity we should use to tell about Him who is willing to give eternal life.

"Corrie, what do you think that young man would have said when he heard that one of his good customers had gone to Mr. ten Boom? Do you think that the name of the Lord would be honored? There is blessed money and cursed money. Trust the Lord. He owns the cattle on a thousand hills and He will take care of us."

I felt ashamed and knew that Father was right. I wondered if I could ever have that kind of trust. I remembered myself as a child, when I had to go to school for the first time. My fingers were tight on the railing again, not wanting to go the direction God wanted, only to follow my own stubborn path. Could I really trust Him—with an unpaid bill?

"Yes, Father," I answered quietly. Who was I answering? My earthly father or my Father in heaven?

## The Trivial Things

As I continued working with Father, we both realized that our characters were formed by our job. Watch repairing is a training in patience. How Father helped me when I had difficulties in the work!

"And who in the whole world should I help with more joy than my own daughter," he often said.

The workshop was opened every morning with prayer and Bible reading. If there were problems, we prayed over them together. Father practiced what Paul advised: ". . . whatever happens, make sure that your everyday life is worthy of the Gospel of Christ" (Philippians 1:27 PHILLIPS).

These simple things kept morale high, but also it was such a joy to experience Jesus' victory. He is a Friend who never leaves us alone.

When my hand was not steady and I had to do a very exact work of putting a frail part of a watch—the balance, for instance—into the movement, I prayed, "Lord Jesus, will You lay Your hand on my hand?" He always did, and our joined hands worked securely. Jesus never fails us for a moment.

I experienced the miracle that the highest potential of God's love and power is available to us in the trivial things of everyday life.

# 12

⊸∞∞⊷

# All Is Well ... Until It Rains

I felt a little strange among the people in that room. Most of the women at the meeting of the Christian Union of the Lady Friends of the Young Girl were very dignified, wearing their beautiful black dresses with high collars and long sleeves. *What was I doing here?* I thought. I was suddenly very conscious of my rather low-necked, short-sleeve blouse, which was appropriate for the watchmaker's workshop but a bit out of place for a gathering of the *Union des Amies de la Jeune Fille*.

When one lady began to make her speech, I forgot about myself and listened, as she expressed great warmth and love for girls who needed help and guidance during a time in their lives when there were possibilities for extremes in good or bad.

In Holland, Sunday school classes ended when one was twelve or thirteen years old, and YWCA groups, were designed for girls eighteen or older. In those crucial and formative years between the two age groups, there was nothing organized for them in the Christian world.

Suddenly I felt a finger punching my back and a whispering voice said, "That's work for you, Corrie ten Boom."

I turned around and looked into the kind eyes of Mrs. Bechtold, a dear old lady who had been a friend of Tante Jans.

"No time," I answered, thinking of the house, the shop, the Bible studies in schools. Oh, dear, I was much, much too busy!

"Talk it over with the Lord," Mrs. Bechtold said.

That was exactly what I did when I went to bed that evening.

## Do It

The next day I told Betsie about the meeting and how the Lord had laid it upon my heart to do something about girls in their early teen years. She began to make plans— we had no money, no experience—but we started.

Betsie had taught Sunday school for many years, so it was not difficult for her to get long lists of names of former pupils. She began to talk to her girls about our plans, and in her quiet way she was a tremendous motivator. The first thing we did was to start the Church Walk Club. The youth church on the Bakenessegracht started at ten o'clock Sunday morning, so we met the girls on a bridge at 8:30, had a long walk to the dunes, played there for a while, and then went to church together.

This was a beginning, but we realized that Sunday was not enough. We talked it over with the children and decided that on Wednesday evening we would gather at our usual meeting place on the bridge and walk to Bloemendaal, where some of the wealthy women had said we could use their parks and gardens for games. The grounds of some of those estates were like forest preserves, and it was such a privilege to be able to enjoy them so freely. After each time of fun we would have a talk about the Lord with the girls.

The club grew and grew as girls brought their friends. It began to get around that Tante Kees (my nickname) was "not such a bad sort"—for an adult, that is!

Betsie and I soon realized that we had a serious need for more girls' club leaders. While Betsie gathered names and addresses of former Sunday school pupils, I found my place for selecting prospects was in the shop. When a young lady bought a watch, or brought one in for repairs, I would find myself looking at her and thinking, "Now I wonder if she's a Christian." As I stood behind the counter and she was sitting in front on a chair, I would start to talk about juvenile delinquency, the need of the gospel's reaching the whole world, particularly girls twelve to eighteen years of age.

When one of these young ladies seemed interested, I invited her to our leaders' club. Within a short time we had forty leaders. Soon some of them dropped out when they realized their responsibilities, but when the chaff left, the wheat remained, and we had an enthusiastic, able group of young women.

Once a week the leaders got together, and everyone had to teach the others the games she knew. I instructed them in giving a Bible message with a short story and a thought they could use that week. Whenever questions came up, we talked them over together to find the answer. We brought up our problems in our prayers and didn't depend on our own resources to work a miracle.

These leaders got together a list of former Sunday school girls and told them about the clubs, where to meet on the bridge, and the name of the park or garden where they would have their game and talk club.

What a beginning we had! It was dynamic—until the rainy month of August started and the entire H.M.C. (*Haarlemse Meisjes Clubs* or Haarlem Girls' Clubs) consisted of dripping-wet leaders who waited in vain on the bridge for the girls who didn't come. We had too many fair-weather girls! We could have given up at that point, but most of us believed if the Lord had directed us into this work, that he wanted us to go on! We were dampened but not drowned!

What we needed was a roof over our heads, and we found a room in a house on the Bakenessegracht. It was close to the Beje, and when supper was over, it took me only a few minutes to run to a meeting. On some Wednesday evenings we had a room jammed with girls, and at other times the place was empty. It was during the "empty" time that our leaders' training club became our leaders' prayer group; we asked the Lord to give us a clubhouse instead of just a club room.

Every city has its famous benefactors, and in Haarlem the name of Teyler was well known. Stories of his wealth, the organizations he had endowed, and his reputation as a promoter of Dutch art were renown. One of the many houses owned by Mr. Teyler had a very large room with many smaller ones around it; from a family viewpoint, it was not a practical home. We asked the regent of the property if we could rent the house—and because we were going to use it for good moral purposes, our offer was quickly accepted. What an answer to prayers!

We had the time of our lives! As we planned together with the girls, they all expressed their different areas of interest. One of the girls, for instance, wanted to learn English. The next week we had an English class started in one of the smaller rooms. The leader of that class was one of our customers in the shop.

The one thing we couldn't do in the Teyler house was the vigorous physical activity that some girls wanted. So for one evening a week we rented a gymnastic hall in Haarlem with all of the equipment we needed. There we started the athletic clubs for the more adventurous.

God blessed the work. Yes, we made mistakes, but in spite of our blunders, the clubs grew in numbers and in strength.

As a result of my association with those women who had given me that first inspiration, we were made a part of the Christian Union of the Lady Friends of the Young Girl, with international headquarters in Switzerland. Our board of directors consisted of dignified ladies, most of them from the upper strata of society and very strict in their opinions. However, they had a healthy sense of humor and astonishing flexibility, considering their background.

One of the areas of real challenge for the board was a young spinster with exploding ideas. Her name was Corrie ten Boom. A doctor's wife, Mrs. Burkens, was given the job of "controlling" Corrie and protecting the larger group from adventures that were considered too dangerous.

### Taboo!

Everything went very well with the board, until I came up with an idea that was revolutionary. I wanted to start a club with boys and girls together! Such a thing was unheard of for a Christian organization; boys belonged in boys' clubs, and girls in girls' clubs, especially during the time of puberty.

Dating had no place in the Christian society; however, a boy and a girl would meet each other in the streets, in secret. After all, I knew a little bit about that—and I will never forget Tante Jans's written tracts after she saw girls flirting in the Barteljorisstraat: *"Jonge Meisjes, Scharrelt Niet!"* ("Young Girls, Don't Flirt!").

The reason we considered having a club for both boys and girls was because the girls themselves were having such fun together that we began to be concerned that we were raising a spinster society. The leaders' group thought if we started a coed club, girls would feel free to invite a boyfriend to the club meeting and wouldn't have to resort to seeing him in secrecy.

I'll never forget the board meeting when I announced that we were starting such a group.

"Corrie, what would some of the parents think?"

"It's never been done before!"

"Corrie, you really surprise us!"

I think I really surprised myself. I pleaded and argued that this was such a good opportunity for real fellowship between the sexes. The only possibility for boys and girls to be with each other was to either meet in the streets, or in the case of bad weather, to meet in the pubs.

I won the battle. However, the board left me with one restriction: For one entire year nobody was allowed to tell about our experiment. At the end of that critical first year, if we didn't have any real problems, we were allowed more publicity. So we started the *Vriendenkring* (The Club of Friends). It may not have been a very clever title, but it was a very popular club. The secrecy of its beginning increased its popularity.

Each evening program of the Friends' Club was unique. My first question was, "Well, what will we do this evening?" Sometimes they discussed rowing on the Spaarne River, but more often the topics centered around politics or the service of the Lord. Somehow young people do not seem to have the same aversion to these topics as their elders.

We had young men of many persuasions; some were communists, while others loved our country and our queen. Many were faithful church members; others were agnostics or atheists. We had no requirements for joining the clubs, and if they didn't like the short Bible talks, they didn't have to listen.

Once the mixed club decided to climb the tower of the cathedral. I'll never forget how I felt as we climbed the highest steps on the outside of the tower and came into the middle of the pinnacle. I looked down upon the *grote markt*, which blossomed with the wares of the farmers and merchants three times a week, and probably wondered what it would be like to land in a bin of onions!

It was the first and last time I ever gathered courage for such an experiment. Going down was almost a greater nightmare than climbing up, and I may have considered (if I had time) the reason why the Lord was putting me through such a test of courage.

Boys and girls found each other in the club, and marriage feasts were high points for all of us. Some were married in churches but later told me, "We have forgotten what the minister said, but the things you taught us in the club feast we understood much better and have remembered them."

## Family Leadership

I had an area of concern about the mixed clubs, and that was my own feeling of inadequacy. I knew that the club-house needed a director, a substitute father and mother, and I certainly was not equipped for either position. We prayed about it, and out of the *Vriendenkring* came just the right couple.

Wim was a tailor from a family of tailors. His father, brother, and Wim's girlfriend, Fie, worked together in their business. They were such a joy to be around—they loved life and especially liked to celebrate with music. The first days of each week they devoted all of their time to developing their musical interests. The walls of their small tailor shop were covered with musical instruments, such as violins, guitars, and mandolins—even the little nine-year-old daughter joined in the family orchestra.

I had to take one of Father's suits in for alteration one Monday morning, and was invited to sit down and listen to their concert. I was their only audience on that day and after almost an hour, I said, "How long do your concerts last?"

"Oh, we play from eight in the morning until eleven at night most of the time on the first four days of the week."

I wasn't used to this lack of work schedule. "But what about your tailoring business?" I asked.

"Most of the time we start that on Thursday . . . sometimes earlier, sometimes later. That depends on . . ."

Their mother finished the sentence, ". . . how much we have to eat in the house!"

My business sense was aroused. "Do your customers agree with this long waiting time when they have ordered a suit or a dress?"

"They don't have to wait long," Wim answered. "When we work, all four of us work together. Fie works with us too." He looked at her with love and pride. "Soon, Tante Corrie, we'll get married and then we are going to live in her room."

I knew Fie's room; it was just an attic in a large apartment house. *Not a very pleasant place to begin married life,* I thought.

"Well, the room is cheap," Wim said when he saw my concerned face.

"Wim . . . Fie . . . I have an idea. Let's talk about it."

Fie was not only a member of our Friends' Club, she was also a perfect leader of several of the girls' clubs. That Monday morning, in the tailor shop temporarily turned concert hall, we began to dream. If Wim and Fie could live in the big clubhouse and be the directing couple for the H.M.C., not only would some of *their* immediate problems be solved, but it would also establish a permanent chaperone on the premises, which would quiet some of the criticisms we had heard.

Wim and Fie moved in and faithfully directed our clubhouse for many years. They became known as "Uncle Wim and Aunt Fie," and later their baby daughter became the youngest member of the H.M.C.

All of my spare time was devoted to the clubs. Father and I experienced ups and downs in the watchmaking business, but each evening I always had one or two clubs to attend. When I came home, Betsie and Father were always longing to hear what I had experienced. They were our prayer partners, and we knew that the Beje was home base for prayer support for all the work in the clubs. How we rejoiced together when people who came to the clubs gave their first yes to Jesus!

About forty years later I returned to Holland after tramping around the world; in a church one day, I met a man who came to me and asked, "Don't you know me? In your *Vriendenkring* I found the Lord. He has never failed me."

Another time a minister saw me in his church and said from the pulpit, "In your club, Corrie, I learned to appreciate the Bible as the living Word of God."

I praised the Lord and chuckled to myself—it was certainly worth the year of being "on trial" and that terrifying climb up the cathedral tower to hear testimonies like that!

# 13

## The Red Cap Club

The quiet years of the early 1920s in our home were punctuated by the sound of Tante Anna's fading alto voice, singing the great old hymns of the church. As the once-vigorous body became weaker, she stayed in bed most of the time, memorizing verse after verse from her worn hymnal. She knew most of the songs slightly, but now learned all the words from the first to the last line. "I've never had time to memorize," she said, "and it's such a joy."

She knew that her time on earth was limited, but she seemed determined to enter heaven with a song on her lips.

When a day in the shop had been particularly difficult, or someone had come to the house burdened with heavy sorrow, it was an encouragement to hear from the little bedroom upstairs the beautiful words:

He leadeth me, O blessed thought!
O words with heavenly comfort fraught!
What e'er I do, where e'er I be,
Still 'tis God's hand that leadeth me.

After a short, severe illness, God led Tante Anna to her new home in heaven. Father, Betsie, and I sat at the big oval table, once so crowded with all the ten Booms, and talked about the past.

"It's a new life now, Corrie; we must remember the past but live in anticipation of the future."

Who could be despondent around Father? His positive attitude enlivened the dullest day. I looked at the empty chairs and began to dream a bit. Mother had always encouraged us in our dreams. I recalled the time Betsie and I had gone to her with an idea we had.

"Mama, when we grow up we want to help children of missionaries. So many of them can't stay with their parents on the mission field, and then they are sent back to Holland to live in those big places where missionary children have their home."

We had recently visited one of those houses, and although the leaders were kind, we felt so sorry for the boys and girls who had to sacrifice because their parents were obeying God by serving in other countries.

I remember how Mother brightened at the thought. She had just left the hospital after a minor operation and told us about a talk she had with the head nurse.

"My nurse had been a missionary for years and when she heard that I had three daughters she said, 'Mrs. ten Boom, I think you should keep one daughter at home, one should be a deaconess in our hospital, and one you should give to the missions.'"

My eyes grew big at the thought. Which one was I to be?

"What was your answer, Mama?"

"I told the nurse—I would not know if I could give a daughter of mine for the mission field!"

Mother explained the reason for her strong feelings.

She continued her story: "My own mother was in Indonesia when she was a little child. Her parents lived there, and both died on the same day. There were three small children left without parents. A black woman took them all to her home and cared for them for two years before they could find a ship with a captain who was willing to take the three orphans to Holland on his ship, without grown-ups to supervise them. The kind people who kept my mother and her brother and sister were very good to them, but my mother's childhood was very primitive. If you wish to serve the Lord by educating missionary children, I believe it would be a very worthwhile pursuit, Corrie."

That story and my dream soon leaped into reality. The meanderings of my mind were interrupted by Willem's familiar voice downstairs. "Is anybody home?"

He told us he had something important to tell us, so Betsie, Father, and I gathered in the parlor. Willem began by saying, "As you know, I'm a board member of the Salatiga Dutch East Indies mission."

Oh, dear, was Willem going to go to the mission field?

But that wasn't it at all. His request, I admit, was a strange "coincidence"—coming at that particular time.

"There are three children of missionaries," Willem continued, "who need to have a home on short notice. Their parents must leave for the mission field. They're very clever children, two girls and a boy. Now we can find a home for the boy, but not for the girls. They all need to study, but there isn't much money."

(That was a familiar phrase in our house.)

"This is a faith mission," Willem explained. "When the finances are good the parents can pay; but if there is nothing, then the foster parents must live on faith like the missionaries. I thought perhaps it could be something for you."

"We'll pray about it, Willem," Father replied, pulling on his beard as he did when he was deep in thought.

Willem knew that he couldn't press Father into a decision before prayer; that was the way decisions were made in our family. However, after supper and prayer, I cleared the dishes from the table as Betsie poured milk into the steaming cups of coffee and Father lit a cigar.

"One girl could sleep in Tante Bep's room," I suggested.

"So, you are already arranging the house," Father chuckled. "If you two agree, I will not refuse. However . . ." and Father paused, perhaps beginning to think of the foolishness of a man in his sixties with two unmarried daughters, taking the responsibility of raising young children. ". . . let's not decide too quickly about this."

The next day the mission director visited us.

"Mr. ten Boom . . . ladies," and he bowed gallantly to us, "the board of the missions met last night and thanked the Lord that you are willing to take the two girls."

Father smiled. "Who told you that? Of course, if you have already thanked God, we cannot refuse. When can the children come that we may see them?"

"Tomorrow."

Betsie and I began to rearrange closets, prepare beds, and plan meals before any of us had a chance to question our decision. It was quite clear to us that the Lord meant for us to take the girls, but we hadn't counted on the added surprise in the missionary package.

The next day three children came: Puck, a spirited

little girl of eleven, Hans, a twelve-year-old with great intelligence, and Hardy, their fourteen-year-old brother. We loved them from the beginning, responding immediately to their bright minds and willingness to adapt to a new way of life. When they were small, they were educated in Indonesia, where their parents served on the mission field; but when they grew older they were sent back to their home country to boarding school, or to live with families. Naturally, the children preferred families to the schools, so they were eager to please.

We showed Puck and Hans to their rooms, and they began to unpack their few belongings from the little cloth satchels they brought with them. Hardy stayed in the kitchen, looking down at the floor.

"Come along, Hardy, it's time for us to leave," the mission director said.

"Sir," Hardy said softly, looking from Father to the director, "can't I stay in this house with the bearded old man? I had to say good-bye to Mom and Dad; I don't want to say good-bye to Hans and Puck too."

Father said, "Of course you are staying, young man. You don't think I can run this household full of women all alone, do you?"

And then we were six.

Our quiet, thin little three-story house was suddenly stretching its walls and echoing the activity of three children. The side door swung in and out like the pendulum on one of our clocks, and it was a good sound. Father seemed to increase his productivity with all the chatter and singing going on around him; the entire tempo of our lives picked up.

Betsie and I discussed the division of labor, and it was settled that she would take care of their clothing and food, and I would be responsible for sports and music. I could combine that with my club work. The first thing I did when the children came was to sell my bicycle. I decided to walk a great deal with them, and as long as we didn't have enough money for bicycles for everyone, I intended to train myself and the children to walk where we had to go.

The Alpina watch company had sent us little red caps—the type worn by the Swiss yodelers—and I gave each of the children one of these. The first time we all ventured out on a walk, the conductor of the street car saw us and said, "Well, here comes Corrie and her Red Cap Club."

We bobbed along the streets of Haarlem and out to the dunes for our hikes, but it wasn't long before there were more red caps added to our little "club."

### Along Comes Lessie

Just as we had the children of the watchmakers come to live with us after the First World War, we inherited another girl who had been promised a home in Holland and then had been rejected. Lessie was a missionary's daughter, who was on a boat ready to sail from Indonesia to Holland, when a telegram came from the uncle she was going to visit, saying that she was not welcome. Her mother was so upset because Lessie needed a time in Holland to begin the training school for teachers, and all the arrangements had been made.

"The parents of Hans and Puck were at the ship—bidding Lessie good-bye," they said. "They always have room, but if they don't they'll make it."

Consequently, we received a letter announcing the

arrival of Lessie within two days. There was no time to write our answer; in fact, there was no alternative.

"We have no room for more beds," Betsie said. Her precise nature of housekeeping was straining with the increasingly crowded and cluttered conditions. However, she didn't complain; she moved things, rearranged furniture, and we made do.

"I can sleep in the tower—the place where the suitcases are kept," Hardy said.

A plan was already forming in my mind. "No, we'll put two beds on top of each other in my room." I invented a type of bunk beds with our old bedsteads.

When Lessie arrived, hurt because she had been refused by her one relative, she was welcomed by us with open arms.

Within a short time the Lord chose to send us two more girls. We experienced that with men there are impossible situations and circumstances, but with God all things are possible.

Our Red Cap Club added more caps, and we began to look like a troop of yodelers!

All the girls went into the training school for teachers, and Hardy went to another school, just for boys. Poor Hardy, he was surrounded by girls, and I'm sure he must have felt overwhelmed at times. He began to disappear for several hours at a time, and one day Betsie marched into the kitchen with a frown on her gentle face.

"Do you know what Hardy is doing?"

*Oh, dear.* I began to imagine all sorts of evil things, none of which seemed to suit Hardy's basic good character.

"He's going to Charlie Chaplin movies!" Betsie announced indignantly.

"To the movies? You don't say!"

None of us had ever been to the movies, but somehow I didn't hold as scandalous a view of this new invention as Betsie did. We didn't forbid Hardy from this pursuit, but we tried to make the activities for the children so attractive that they weren't too interested in such things.

I loved the physical activities with my foster children. When we walked together, we talked together, and it was more valuable than any "lectures" we might give. We had such great fun on our hikes. Once we walked with one of my clubs from Haarlem to Amsterdam, which was a distance of seventeen kilometers (about ten miles). We carried our lunch and sang whenever our spirits began to droop a bit. My foster children were the most enthusiastic.

We had gymnastic lessons too, although I wasn't a very good pupil myself. My feet never seemed to do what my mind instructed them. We all worked out on the gymnastic bars, with a succession of teachers who taught their individual type of body movements; the German method taught a different style from the French, and both were contrary to the Swedish gymnastics. I learned to do a bird's nest on the bars, but I was certainly an awkward bird compared to my club girls.

In the middle of a gymnastic lesson, I would blow my whistle and we would have a Bible lesson that would last from two to five minutes. The lessons were usually in the form of stories that the children could remember—stories that emphasized a Bible truth.

For instance, I told the story about the old monk. "There was an old monk who sang a Christmas song every Christmas Eve for his brothers in the monastery and for visitors who would come from the village for the special services. His voice was very ugly, but he loved the Lord and sang from his heart. Once the director of the cloister said, 'I'm sorry, Brother Don, we have a new monk who has such a beautiful voice . . . he will sing this Christmas.'

"The man sang so beautifully that everyone was happy.

"But that night an angel came to the superior and said, 'Why didn't you have a Christmas Eve song?'

"The superior was very surprised. 'We had a beautiful song, didn't you hear it?'

"The angel shook his head sadly, 'It may have been very inspiring to you, but we didn't hear it in heaven.'

"You see, the old monk with the raspy voice had a personal relationship with the Lord Jesus, but the young monk was singing for his own benefit, not for that of the Lord's."

"That's a good story, Tante Kees," Puck panted while trying to do a backbend and talk at the same time. (She called me by the nickname that all the club girls used.) "Is that in the Bible?"

"No, Puck, but the Bible does say, 'but if anyone loves God, he is known by Him' (1 Corinthians 8:3). Do you think that God knew the young monk?"

The girls were in a training school for teachers, and the quick little Bible studies in story form came in very handy for them.

One day they told us about a student in their class who cried a lot. Hans was especially concerned about her, and at supper time, while everyone was around the oval table, she brought up the subject.

"Remember me telling you about Miep, the girl in our class who cries a lot? Well, I talked to her today during recess and found out that she lives with a cousin. Her parents are in Belgium. She can't seem to eat. Anyhow, her cousin told her that she had to finish her meal before she could leave for school, so she's almost always late. She's miserable with her cousin and doesn't want to go back."

"Please, Tante Betsie, Tante Kees, take Miep into our house," Puck said. "She's really so sweet but so unhappy. We can sleep two in a bed."

The next day, Betsie went to visit the cousin and his wife. They were good people but had very little insight about raising a teenager. They agreed that we should have Miep in our house for a time.

When Miep arrived, Betsie gave her a real welcome. "Look, Miep, no one here has to eat who doesn't want to . . . here is the bread; whenever you are hungry, you can help yourself and make a sandwich."

Miep soon became a happy, relaxed girl, full of humor and a good, normal appetite.

With seven children in the house now, the Beje was an active, noisy place. In the evenings Father sat in the living room, surrounded by his second family, busily writing his weekly paper. He went about his work oblivious to the din surrounding him, looking up occasionally to smile at one of the children.

The girls were always in a hurry to get to one of their clubs or to do their studying. They tried to shorten the devotions at night, but Father, called Opa by the children, was aware of their methods.

Puck said once, "Opa, let's just read Psalm 117 tonight."

"Well, now, Puck, I just think I'll read Psalm 119."

A visitor commented to Father that he was astonished at all the noise and laughter in our house. Father said, "Our children are such good kids . . . why they never quarrel and are always ready to help each other. They're just angels."

I sighed and went upstairs to talk to Puck, who had been sent to her room for the "angelic" way she had said, "I hate Lessie!"

She was sitting in the corner of her bed, curled up in that defiant position children take when they know they're going to be punished.

"Puck, don't you know that Jesus says hatred is murder in God's eyes. He told us that we must love our enemies," I said.

"Well, I can't love Lessie!"

"In Romans 5:5 Paul says, '. . . the love of God has been poured out within our hearts through the Holy Spirit who was given to us.' If you give room in your heart for the Holy Spirit, He will give you His love, a part of the fruit of the Spirit—and that love never fails."

Puck looked up, a trace of tears in her eyes, "But, Tante Kees, what must I do? Such hateful thoughts come in my heart."

"John says, 'If we confess our sins, he is faithful and just to forgive us our sins, and to cleanse us from all unrighteousness' (1 John 1:9 KJV). Jesus will cleanse your heart with His blood, and then He will fill you with His love. Shall we go to Him now and tell Him everything?"

Puck relaxed. All the tension in her taut muscles left, and she lowered her head as we prayed together. Puck and Lessie became the greatest of friends. Years later, Puck was in a concentration camp in Indonesia, placed there by the Japanese during World War II. The guards were very cruel, and how she needed the Holy Spirit to give her love for her enemies! She was married then, and her husband, Fritz, was in a concentration camp in the Philippines.

When she was released she only weighed seventy-nine pounds. Fritz survived the years of imprisonment and was an emaciated 106 pounds when he was freed.

Puck told me after the war, "I always thought if I came out alive, 'I wonder if my parents in Holland will have the strength to stand the hardships of the war—but I know that Opa and Tante Betsie and Tante Kees will be there.' That gave me a feeling of security. When I was beaten, I thought of you and Opa and remembered what you had taught me about love for my enemies."

Puck's parents were still alive when she came back after the war. Opa and Tante Betsie were no longer there, but what they had taught Puck lasted. "The righteous shall be in everlasting remembrance" (Psalm 112:6 KJV).

Although Betsie and I never married, we received such love from all of our children and were able to give them so much of our love! However, a house full of teenagers was not uncomplicated. There were many things to talk over with the Lord. Daily. Sometimes there was not much money. When they needed new shoes they had to wait until the finances were available. Cardboard or newspapers temporarily stuffed in the soles were frequent emergency measures.

We shared our sorrows and joys with all of them. When I sold an expensive clock or watch, I came to the living room, stood in the door, and made an impressive announcement.

"Ladies—and the two gentlemen present—I wish to inform all of you gathered for this important occasion that Mrs. van der Hoeven has just purchased the gold Alpina, and paid cash for it!"

Cheers. Hurrahs.

"Now I can get my shoes."

"And I my petticoat."

When the situation was serious, we prayed about it and didn't forget afterward to thank God together. We lived as a real family.

Betsie was wonderful in contacting the parents; she wrote them every week. When one of the girls got a new dress, she took a snapshot and sent it to the parents together with a piece of material.

Marijke was the only girl who had difficulties in school. She was studying to be a kindergarten teacher and loved children but was terrified of examinations. Once she failed, and it was difficult to persuade her to go back the next time.

She adored Opa—as all the children did. The evening before the crucial day of the examination, he was writing his weekly paper and concentrating so intently that it was almost impossible to stir him, except with something very tempting.

He laid down his pen when Puck brought in the tea. She had made cookies, and everyone had to pay attention to such a treat.

"I'm not going to the examination tomorrow," Marijke stated.

"Why not?" Father asked, immediately concerned over one of his children.

"I'll fail again."

Father smiled. "Listen, Marijke, you have done your best and possibly you can't do it alone. But Paul said, 'I can do all things through Christ who strengthens me.' Do you think He will give you strength if you trust Him?"

"Paul never had to go to examinations," Hardy remarked with the complete assurance of a teenage boy who knows all the answers.

"I think his questioning from Felix was a bit tougher than an exam for a kindergarten teacher," Lessie answered, pleased with herself for making this comparison. (We had been studying the Book of Acts.)

"Can you really pray for everything? Even something as little as an examination?" Marijke asked with renewed interest.

Father leaned back in his chair, warming his hands with the steaming tea, relishing the chance to discuss the Scriptures. "Paul says in Philippians 1:27, 'Whatever happens make sure that your everyday life is worthy of the gospel of Jesus Christ.' When you belong to the Lord, there's not one single thing you have to conquer in your own strength. The hairs of your head are numbered; can anything be more trivial than that?"

"But, Opa," Puck said, "yesterday I didn't learn French because I was busy making the cookies. That was more fun than dull old French. So this morning I prayed that I wouldn't be called on. But God didn't help me. I did get called on—and what a mess I made of the French words!"

"I'm not surprised," Father chuckled. "If you didn't learn, you can't expect the Lord to help you."

Hardy added, with a sudden burst of understanding that made me very pleased with him, "I've found out that if I want to pray for something that is wrong, I simply can't."

It was years later that I had to learn another lesson about prayer for something that was not one hundred percent right.

It was in 1945, shortly after the war, that I went to Switzerland. I had spoken there in many meetings, but also I visited my former watchmaker friends from whom I had learned my trade many years before. I bought some watches while I was there. In Holland, there was still a severe shortage of imported articles and to buy Swiss watches was rather complicated.

When I put my watches in my suitcase, I smiled because of the methods we had learned in the time of the underground work when we saved Jewish people and hid articles in our luggage. Surely nobody should be able to find my three watches!

Before I went to the train, I prayed the way I always do when I start a trip.

"Lord, protect us against accidents, bless the engineer of the train and give him wisdom, make us a blessing for our fellow travelers, and Lord . . . give us success in smuggling . . . in smug. . . ." (I wanted to say, "In smuggling my watches," but I couldn't.)

The moment I started to pray for it, I knew it was a sin. Smuggling to avoid paying money is the same as stealing. I didn't smuggle my watches, and I experienced again that prayer can be a discipline. Praying for something that is wrong is not possible.


As the girls grew older and discovered that boys were more than just a nuisance, it became an increasing challenge to answer their questions. The walks we had together brought a closeness and ease of communication, in spite of our difference in age. Usually we walked on Sunday afternoon, since our week was filled with work and school. I remember when we walked from Haarlem to the dunes near Zandvoort, the sun warm on our faces and the sand inviting us to sunbathe, we would frequently lie on our backs and talk about . . . well, just the things girls talk about.

"Tante Kees, were you ever engaged to be married?"

"Tante Kees, do you long to have a husband? Do you find it difficult to be single?"

Once they started, the girls could ask questions as rapidly as a second hand could move in an accurate timepiece.

"You rascals . . . this is a very important subject to talk about when you are beginning your lives as young women." I had no sadness or regret, only joy in telling the story of Karel.

"There was a time in my life when I expected to marry a boy who loved me and whom I loved. He was going to be a minister and was from a big family where several members were clergymen. They had the usual problems that ministers have with finances.

"His mother did not approve of our getting married. She wanted him to marry a rich girl.

"How I struggled with myself at that time! When he introduced me to the wealthy girl he was going to marry, I had the feeling that my heart would never survive such a blow."

"What did you do, Tante Kees?"

"I went to my room and talked it over with the Lord. From what I can remember it was something like this: 'I want, Lord, to belong to You with my body, soul, and mind. I claim Your victory, Lord Jesus, over that wound which is hurting me. Let Your victory be demonstrated also in my sex life.'

"I didn't quite analyze what I needed, but the joy is that with the Lord, it is not necessary to give Him a clear diagnosis before He knows the cure."

"Did you have an immediate victory?"

"No, there was still a battle—rather severe—but then the Lord healed me and the pain didn't come back. The Lord gave and continues to give me a very happy life. I have the love of all of you—and I love you. My life isn't dull at all. The best thing is that when Jesus restores such a loss, He gives a fulfillment that is a little bit of heaven— a peace that passes all understanding. From our side it is only necessary to surrender."

After I had told this, Puck said, "Now I understand more what Opa said yesterday: 'Our times are in His hands.'"

## He Brings You Safely Home

It was the middle of May 1940. By that time the children were all away in their different jobs or married. It was a time of fear and confusion in our land.

Hitler and Goering had ordered a heavy bombing of Rotterdam—and we were bewildered! The Dutch experienced the first large-scale airborne attack in the history of warfare.

We were completely unprepared for such an ordeal. On the morning of May 14, 1940, a German staff officer crossed the bridge at Rotterdam with a white flag in his hand and demanded the surrender of the city. He warned that unless it capitulated, it would be bombed.

While surrender negotiations were actually under way, the bombers appeared and wiped out the heart of our great city. Over eight hundred persons, mostly civilians, were massacred; several thousand were wounded, and seventy-eight thousand homeless. Rotterdam surrendered and then the Dutch armed forces did the same. It was then our dear Queen Wilhelmina and the government members fled to London.

The German juggernaut was on the move. An army of tanks larger in size, concentration, and striking ability than any tank force yet mobilized started through the Ardennes Forest from the German frontier. We read that these tanks stretched three columns wide, for a hundred miles behind the Rhine, and broke through the French armies headed for the English Channel.

Our Hans was married by then and had two children and another one on the way. Her husband was a teacher, and they lived in Rotterdam during that terrible bombardment. They fled to a small suburb of Rotterdam, where her third baby was born in a cellar. For a year they lived in that cellar, which formed a bomb shelter.

Hans told me in later years that over and over again she repeated to her children, "Opa taught us, 'When Jesus takes your hand, He keeps you tight. When Jesus keeps you tight, He leads you through your whole life. When Jesus leads you through your life, He brings you safely home.'"

# 14

Even the Least of Them . . .

In addition to the work in the business, the club work, and the care for our children, I continued with the Bible lessons in the schools. One of these classes was for children who had learning difficulties. It was such a joy to know that the Holy Spirit doesn't need a high IQ in a person in order to reveal Himself. Even people of normal or superior intelligence need the Lord to understand the spiritual truths that are only spiritually discerned.

God gave me a great love for the "exceptional children." I remember going to these schools and telling Bible stories and being rewarded when their faces lit up with sweet and simple happiness.

Sometimes I asked them questions to see if they understood what I told them. Once a feebleminded girl answered a question of mine that might have baffled a person of normal intelligence. I asked, "What is a prophet and what is a priest?"

She said, "They are both messengers between God and man."

I continued, "Then they are the same—a prophet and a priest?"

She thought awhile and then answered, "No, a prophet

has his back to God and his face to us—and a priest has his face to God and his back to us."

I wasn't sure if she had learned that by heart, so I asked her, "Well, what was I today?"

She said, "You were both—you told us about God and you were a prophet. Then you prayed. You didn't pray for yourself, but you prayed for us—then you were a priest."

That was a backward child who answered in that manner! When you bring the gospel, it is the Holy Spirit who works.

I tried to teach these children other things with much less success; one time I started to instruct them about the stars. I brought some white beans to school and laid them on the table in the form of constellations. I showed them Orion, and they looked at the formation of the beans, and all of them knew it very well. Then one evening I took them outside and said, "Look, children, there is Orion . . . see it?"

They just shook their heads. "No, Tante Corrie, they are white beans in the sky."

They never understood what I told them about the stars, but the truths of the Lord they seemed to understand well.

Whenever you come in contact with feebleminded people, please tell them that Jesus loves them. They often understand God's love better than people who have problems because of their intellectual doubt.

Paul wrote in 1 Corinthians 1:20–21: "Where is the wise man? Where is the scribe? Where is the debater of this age? Has not God made foolish the wisdom of the world? For since in the wisdom of God the world through its wisdom did not come to know God, God was well-pleased through the foolishness of the message preached to save those who believe."

## Some Are Forgotten

Father shared my concern, my outreach for the debilitated and the disturbed. Once he heard from a servant girl about a woman in a mental hospital who never received a visit from anyone.

Father, Betsie, and I prayed for this woman, and then I made the trip to the hospital. It took me some hours to go there, and when I finally found the woman, I discovered that she was clear in her thinking, although a bit mentally disturbed. Also her body was sick, and she couldn't leave her bed.

"May I introduce myself? I'm Corrie ten Boom. I've come to visit you," I said.

She looked up at me with tears of joy in her eyes.

"Did God send you?"

"Yes, I'm sure He did . . . and I'm glad too, because I would like you to be my friend. Will you?"

"Oh, yes," she said eagerly. "Will you please visit me sometimes? Can you tell me about Jesus?"

I thought for a moment. How much did this woman know? What Bible story could help her? I prayed for inspiration and then told her about the good shepherd who brought the lost sheep home.

We became real friends, in spite of being such an unequal combination! There I was, a healthy, normal girl, and she was an older woman with a confused mind. I truly believe the Lord brought us together.

Often in the midst of a very busy workday, with the

watch repairs stacked on the counter waiting to be done, Father would say to me, "Why don't you visit Alida today? She's come into my mind . . . perhaps she is lonely."

Dear Papa! It meant more work for him because a visit to this friend of mine took at least four hours of the day.

On one visit we talked at some length about heaven. Two days later the nurse at the hospital called me on the phone. "Alida has died suddenly. Can you give us the address of her relatives?"

I know that tears came to my eyes, but I could thank the Lord that she was now with Him in the beautiful heaven we had so recently talked about. "I'm sorry," I told the nurse, "I don't know anything about Alida's relatives."

"But you were such a close friend," she replied.

"I asked her once if she had sisters and brothers. She told me that years ago they had brought her to the hospital. She had never heard from them again. She didn't know if they were alive, and if so, where they lived."

Father said that evening, "Corrie, I believe that this friendship and the time you gave that poor woman has shown God's loving kindness for the despised and lost more than any other work you have done. I'm sure it was important in God's eyes."

## Just a Boy Named Henk

Henk was a boy who was a member of my Bible class for mentally retarded. He came from a family with eleven children, and it was difficult for his poor tired mother to give him much attention.

It was from this simple little boy that I saw again how the Holy Spirit reveals himself in such a marvelous way to low-IQ people.

Once I visited Henk at home, and his mother received me with such a thankful manner. "Henk talks so much about the stories you tell in his Bible class. He never remembers anything about any other class, but when he comes from your class he talks to his brothers and sisters about it."

"Is Henk at home?"

"He's in his room upstairs . . . in the corner of the attic. He's there most of the time . . . he's really my easiest boy. We know he'll never become a professor or anything important, but he does work for a salary—he's in a government workshop where he makes clothespins the whole day. Dear Henk, he's so satisfied, but when he's at home the house is so full of noise that he goes to his attic room."

I went upstairs and found Henk on his knees in front of a chair. Before him was an old dirty picture of Jesus on the cross. I stopped at the door to listen, for Henk was singing. His voice was soft and hoarse.

Out of my bondage, sorrow and night,
    Jesus, I come, Jesus, I come;
Into Thy freedom, gladness and light,
    Jesus, I come to Thee.
Out of the depths of ruin untold,
    into the peace of Thy sheltering fold,
Ever Thy glorious face to behold,
    Jesus, I come to Thee.

I've heard Bach played by Schweitzer, and anthems sung by gigantic choirs, but at that moment I felt as if I were in a cathedral with angels surrounding me. I tiptoed back downstairs without disturbing him, praising God again for the love He brings into the lives of "even the least of them."

Some time later I heard that Henk's mother had gone into his attic room and found him before the chair, with the picture of Jesus in his hand. Henk was home with the Lord. When I heard about his death I wondered if he had been singing, "Jesus, I come to Thee" at that last moment.

## Thirty Years Later

It was after World War II and I was working in East Germany, teaching the gospel in a huge cathedral. I went into a counseling area to talk with people individually; there were many more who needed help waiting outside in another room. I heard a very noisy discussion; everyone seemed to be talking too loudly at the same time. Suddenly everything was quiet and I heard an unusually tender, beautiful voice singing. It was Henk's hymn in German: "Out of my bondage, sorrow and night, Jesus, I come."

I opened the door into the room where the inquirers were waiting and saw a child of about fourteen years of age. Her face was like an angel, and there was something so moving about her that many in the room were crying. The girl's mother stood beside her and held her hand.

When they came into the inquiry room, I found out that the girl's name was Elsa, and I realized immediately that she was not a normal child.

"Where did you learn that song, Elsa?" I asked her gently.

"In prison . . . a man taught it to me, and I sang it every day."

"Why was Elsa in prison?" I asked her mother.

"My husband is a communist. Elsa is mentally retarded. She loves the Lord Jesus and speaks about Him frequently, but her father is an atheist and a leader in his party, so he had no difficulty putting Elsa in prison. A short while ago we got her out . . . it was so terribly cold in that jail that the guards themselves helped me get Elsa out. They heard and enjoyed her singing, and Elsa was always ready to tell them about her Lord."

My lips quivered as I held Elsa's hands, and I remembered so many things . . . the Bible studies in Holland . . . Henk in his attic room . . . and what Father had often said to me. "Corrie, what you do among these people is of little importance in the eyes of men, but I'm sure in God's eyes it is the most valuable work of all."

# 15

⚬⚭⚬

# Leaders and Blunders

I loved the activity—the challenge—the excitement of seeing lives changed. The need in the young people was obvious as the clubs multiplied rapidly.

Once a month we had representatives of every club gather to give suggestions and form plans. We had so many interest groups: handcrafts, sewing, piano, harmonium, choir. As a few girls with other talents expressed the need for another group, we would find a leader and begin another club.

I led the music group myself. Music has always been an important part of my life, and it was such a joy for me to work with these girls. Our club had eight members; seven girls worked at a table on harmony and the study of music, while one went to the piano or organ. Consequently, each member had the lengthy chance of five or ten minutes behind the keyboard.

My, what mistakes I made in that club! If I had taught them watch repair, I would have known exactly what I was doing; but the times that I sent a substitute leader, my lack of real skill in music was glaringly evident! My substitute was Ann, a lady who had many diplomas from the music academy. When she took my organ and piano club, her trained ears suffered—to put it mildly. Dear

Ann, I learned so much from her! She never refused to help me. In her humble and shy way, she lovingly told me of some of the horrible mistakes in instruction I had made. However, she didn't have a critical spirit and was able to correct me in such a loving manner. This was a gift that set such an example for me.

I loved this music club, but the few-minute message was the important part of the evening for me. These short talks about the Lord weren't deep theological studies but stories from the Bible and about the lives of other Christians. They were brief on purpose; some of the club members expected this part of the evening, but it wasn't really their cup of tea. They seemed to endure it for the sake of the fun in the clubs.

We had a theme for everything we did: It was "Him in the Midst of the Clubs." This is exactly what we did—put the message in the middle of the meeting. We knew if we gave it at the beginning, some would avoid it by coming late; if we talked of our theme later in the evening, they left early.

However, many seeds fell upon fertile ground, and when club members began to open their hearts and ask questions about Jesus, we decided to start a Catechism Club. In this group, they could learn enough to become a member of the church. Some called it the Confirmation Club.

I especially loved the Heidelberg Catechism (not all of the fifty-two Sundays, but many of them). I translated the old-fashioned and complicated style of expression into everyday language that my girls could understand. It was amazing how they enjoyed it and how much it became a part of them.

My teaching, however, did not always meet with enthusiasm from the pastors of the churches.

To become a member of the Dutch Reformed Church, there was an examination by the pastor in the presence of elders and deacons. The first time I had just a few confirmands, so the pastor invited me to come together with the new members he had trained. It was an interesting experience.

First the pastor asked one of his pupils a simple question. "Who was the first man in the world?"

Silence. Embarrassment.

He hinted by saying, "It starts with A."

She replied with a proud smile, "That must be Abram."

The pastor was so humiliated.

My pupils studied the Bible and the catechism very hard. The last few weeks before confirmation, they came several evenings to see me and to repeat what they had learned. One of my confirmands was asked, "Do you know the name of one judge of Israel?"

Without hesitation the boy rattled off the names of Othniel, Ehud, Shamgar, Deborah, and the names of the other judges. The examining board was impressed.

One of my girls was asked to tell the story of one of the judges. She said that Gideon was a very shy and bashful man; and when the angel appeared to him, he told Gideon that because the Lord was with him, he was a mighty man of valor. However, she added, "I would never have chosen him to become a hero. I think he was a sissy. But because the Lord was with him, he was mighty."

Later I heard from the French nanny of the minister's little boy that the pastor came home and declared, "I'll never examine Corrie ten Boom's confirmands and mine together again! I've seldom been so ashamed of the poor results of my teaching."

Later it was more than embarrassment, it became a

real collision. I was examining a girl for confirmation and refused to recommend her because she didn't believe that Jesus had died on the cross. She was very unhappy over my decision and said, "I'm not religious like you, but I'd like to become a member of a church. I think it's dignified and I like that. Besides, my mom is going to give me a new dress for the occasion."

I still refused and she went to the minister, who reversed my decision and allowed her to become a church member. He said, "I like the idea of a herd. Some are sheep, some are not—but that doesn't matter."

That minister eventually left the pastorate to become a professor of theology at a university.

## Leadership Training

As the clubs and the work increased, it became obvious that we must devote more time to leadership training. When we had our weekly meetings with our leaders, we took turns telling a story from the Bible while the rest of us criticized. The type of questions we asked were:

Was the gospel clear?
How was her first sentence; did it attract attention?
Was there humor?
What help was there for the girls this week?
What importance did the story have for eternity?
Did she describe colors, movements?
Did she draw clear pictures with good illustrations?
Was it an inspiration for action, for faith, for endurance?

Problems were discussed and then there was prayer. All of us did the work because we loved it; we had so much fun ourselves, but we also understood why it was important. It was a humble little piece of building the kingdom of God.

One of the problems we had was that we didn't have enough able leaders. Another serious one was that it was difficult to get rid of the wrong ones. The most impossible of all the leaders was *Kipslang*. The girls gave her that name because she told the Adam and Eve story by saying that the snake had legs like a chicken. After that her name became Kipslang (chicken-snake).

The girls roared with laughter during her story about Adam and Eve, and she cried with holy indignation over their ridicule. Weren't girls supposed to be serious when listening to a Bible story? Kipslang's club was always a sensation. Girls cried often because of her harsh remarks, and she usually answered by crying also. There was always noise and disorder in her club, and on one occasion the girls began to throw chairs at each other. It was quite out of control, but no other club was as popular because something was always happening there!

It was really remarkable: Once we had ten clubs that all formed as a result of split-ups from Kipslang's club! Dear Kipslang—she was often a headache, but club work certainly prepared her for the future. When I last heard of her, she had been married three years and had just given birth to her second set of twins.

## Let's Go Camping

During the summer we arranged camps that brought girls and leaders closer together than all the weekly meetings. Most of the time we went to the *Bliscap* (an old word for *joy*), which was a simple log cabin with room for about sixty girls.

The campfires were high spots during our outings. There we talked about the Lord, sang hymns, and prayed. The girls were very strict about our campfire time—they were rascals and "born after the fall," but they always said, "At a campfire you look into the flames and listen to God."

In the camps and conferences, one of the biggest dangers was the gossip. We made a camp law and one of the articles was: "If you must tell something negative about someone else, first tell ten positive qualities about him."

If a gossiping remark was made during a meal, we simply said, "Pass the salt, if you please."

Our foster children enjoyed the club and camp life with me. All of them were such a great help to us as leaders, and the love between us made it possible for me to depend upon them for so many tasks. It was always such a joy to have them together with the other club girls. Most of them had such good training that later they were able to do club work wherever they were, scattered over the world.

My girls learned some of the basic lessons of life and death at the camps. Toddy and Janny, sisters, had several real aunts in Holland with whom they spent a part of their vacations. Once in a camp with me, they received a phone call from an uncle that their most beloved aunt had died. They had known that her life was in danger for she was a hemophiliac. When she had a wound, the bleeding wouldn't stop, and upon the birth of her first baby she died. She was very young, and the girls were brokenhearted. It was the first time that someone they loved had been taken from them by death.

"Would you like to go to be with your uncle?" I asked.

"Yes, we would. We couldn't enjoy camp anymore—perhaps we can help with the funeral."

"Tomorrow I'll take you to the train. There's no connection tonight," I explained.

I saw their sad young faces and suggested taking a walk over the heather fields. When we were alone, I let them talk and talk about their aunt. I have found this is one of the most important things to do for a person who is grieving—have him talk about the loved one who is gone. Toddy and Janny knew their aunt loved the Lord and that she had known there was the danger of dying as soon as she had a wound.

I had my little New Testament in the pocket of my uniform and read from Romans 8:28 (KJV). "All things work together for good to them that love God. . . ."

Also, "These little troubles (which are really so transitory) are winning for us a permanent and glorious reward out of all proportion to our pain" (2 Corinthians 4:17 PHILLIPS).

Toddy and Janny confronted the reality and the glory of death that summer at camp. Some years later Toddy married her uncle, which may seem strange, but he was only nine years older than she. They had several children and a good life together.

## Along the River Rhine

One trip (which was unforgettable) was a hiking and camping adventure the club girls had through Germany. All the girls (who could spend the time and money) met each week in our clubhouse to learn the German language. If someone knew a sentence that would be useful when traveling, she would express it to the group, and all the girls would write the sentence in Dutch and in German in their notebooks. Everyone had a little knowledge of the language before we started our trip. I told them the German words and they wrote them down phonetically.

The Rhine River was never so beautiful as it was that summer. I don't believe I've ever enjoyed a trip through a foreign land as much as I did when traveling with girls who had never been outside their country.

Many years later, one of the girls who went on our German trip became seriously ill. In her feverish state, she talked about the only foreign country trip she had ever made; it had been the highlight of her life. However, just the recall of that trip didn't help her when she was treading the valley of the shadow of death. There she was not alone, because Jesus was her Savior. She had given her heart to Him in one of the clubs. This was the most important purpose of our club work: to confront each person with Him, who is our only comfort in life and death.

Jesus is the real security in this world, even in the hour we have to leave it.

### Blunder Boom

Sometimes I think my middle name is *Blunder*. I made some big mistakes, but I can say that our clubs became a success in spite of me. I loved my girls and shared many of their joys and difficulties.

As the years passed and some of our club girls grew older or others wished to join, some of the teenagers didn't like to belong to a club where "older people" came.

"We must make an age limit for our clubs," some experienced club leaders suggested. "Let's make it twenty-five years."

I protested. I had some fine girls who had already passed that age, and I couldn't stand the idea of being forced to send them away.

"I don't think we should have any limit—let's just consider the ages eight to eighty. Why not?"

No one challenged me. When I had a fixed opinion, it was almost impossible to dissuade me; consequently, the age limit was never changed.

One blunder (which may have turned into a blessing) was when I chose a campsite rather close to soldiers' quarters. In their free time, the men showed a great interest in the girls. Of course, the girls returned that interest. That's understandable.

One day during that camp, we marched through the village at the moment the soldiers came off duty. The boys surrounded us on all sides. An officer who had been a daily visitor at the Beje saw our problem. He took his bicycle and rode beside our group, ordering all the soldiers away. Then he escorted us until we reached the camp.

That officer was a blessing to me, but I'm not sure all the girls felt the same way. The campfires became quite a problem. When the girls gathered around the fire, we seemed to have soldiers growing out of the trees. It was very difficult to get any attention from the girls for our talks and singing. I appealed to the officer for help, and he offered: "Every evening I'll send you two trustworthy sergeants to serve as camp watchers. They'll report any soldier who comes within a quarter of a mile of your tents and campfire."

After that two men joined our campfire every evening. They were never the same men, so the rotation system worked very well. They told us later that they enjoyed their "girls' club watch," and there was never a lack of volunteers.

I've sometimes wondered if there was some seed of the gospel sown in the hearts of those men. We never know. God can give a straight blow with a crooked stick. He blesses in spite of our blunders.

# 16

————— ∞ —————

# Safety Pins on Uniforms

We used every method we could think of to recruit girls for our clubs. We took lists from school or church, we talked to shopkeepers, we even placed notices in the newspapers. One of our girls, Annie, answered our advertisement when she was only eleven or twelve years old and remained as a club girl for many years. The advertisement was simple, but it brought results. It read: DO YOU LIKE TO GO ON WALKS? IF YOU WANT TO MEET OTHER GIRLS AND HAVE FUN, COME TO THE TEN BOOM SHOP AT BARTELJORISSTRAAT 19.

The gymnastics club was one of the most popular. I worked out with the girls under the guidance of capable teachers, but I certainly wasn't one of the best pupils. Far from it. My girls were much stronger than I, and how they helped me because of my fain efforts to do some of the exercises.

When the gymnastics club needed a slogan, one of the girls suggested that it should be: WE MAKE STRAIGHT WHAT IS CROOKED. What rascals! They looked at my legs and then at my face to see if I understood what they meant. We had such great fun together. The teasing made for an easier relationship. We were friends, and when I blew my whistle, they all sat down to listen. Most of them knew very little about the Lord Jesus, and several of them freely admitted that they came for fun and not for spiritual matters.

One time I flopped on the floor after trying some new trick on the bars and failing miserably. The girls did their best to help Tante Kees accomplish the simple exercises. I spied Greetje sitting cross-legged in the corner and moved wearily toward her. Then I saw that she was crying, and I asked her if she wanted to tell me what was wrong.

"My older sister Betty is dying. I have learned so much here about Jesus, but I know she doesn't know anything about Him."

"Tell her," I said.

"But how, Tante Kees; I don't know as much as you do."

"Tell her about the cross where Jesus died to carry the punishment that we earned. Tell Betty that Jesus loves her and has said, 'Come to me all'—and that means Betty too."

Greetje began to cry harder, but it was her turn to work out on the bars, so she struggled to get up and wiped away the tears. After she was through she came back to me.

"Then what should I do?"

"Ask Betty if she knows that she is a sinner."

"She knows that."

"Tell her that every sinner may come to Jesus. She must ask forgiveness, and then He will make her heart clear. You know what I told you about that today. She must ask Jesus to come into that clear heart. Let her first say: 'Thank you, Jesus, for dying for me.'"

Greetje went back for another workout. The third

time we talked I said, "Tell Betty that Jesus has said, 'In My Father's house are many mansions . . . I go to prepare a place for everyone who belongs to Me.' When Betty gives her heart to Jesus, she surely belongs to Him."

For several gymnasium evenings, I taught Greetje more about the way to bring Betty to the Lord. After a few weeks, I was invited to come to their home. Greetje greeted me at the door and there was no sign of a distressed little girl. "Tante Kees, come in . . . I want you to see Betty."

Resting on a small bed against the wall was a pale young girl, smiling at me with the radiance only God can give. "Jesus is in my heart . . . He has forgiven me my sins. Greetje told me all about it."

Some days later that girl died, and again I had to speak at a burial. I praised the Lord that my work in gymnastics with the girls—even though awkward at times—had been used to reach someone before it was too late.

Gradually the clubs began to take on more degree of organization. It was exciting to see that this wasn't the case of formation of an organization first, then imposing upon it the concept of girls' clubs—but of the need coming before the structured format.

Out of the gymnastics club, in particular, came the Girl Guide clubs in Holland. The uniforms, slogan, songs, and mottos were gradually added, but only as there was a necessity for them. We did discover, however, that there was a healthy difference between Boy Scouting and Girl Scouting.

One of our gymnast teachers was a scout leader. I asked him what activities he had with the boys that week, and he showed me some games and taught me some knots. *Oh, well*, I thought, *we can do that*. The next day I taught the knots and played games with my Girl Guides. *This is easy! I'll just ask him each week what he does and copy those activities.*

The next week he told me that he had fastened a strong rope on a tree at the top of a dune and strung the rope to another tree some distance away. The boys had to climb along that rope from one end to the other. I listened to this idea, but that day it dawned on my stupid mind that Boy Scouting and Girl Scouting were two different things!

## The End of the World?

One evening I was meeting with a group of pioneers (the older Girl Guides), when Max, one of our faithful members, ran into the room, late and breathless, her voice high with alarm.

"Tante Kees, there's something wrong with the stars! They're running all over the sky, as if they want to see what is happening on the other side of the horizon."

The girls, excitable creatures that they were, jumped up and ran outside. "Why, those are meteors," I said. "Let's go to the Kenaupark and watch from there . . . we can see better."

We ran to the Kenaupark where our beautiful cherry tree The Bride of Haarlem was and watched the exciting display of shooting stars.

Pietje said, "I'm scared . . . is it the end of the world?"

"Girls, those are not stars but meteors, perhaps broken off from other planets. As soon as they enter the earth's atmosphere they are heated and become luminous like a streak of light."

"Pietje, this isn't a sign of the end of the world,

although Jesus has told us that when He comes, one of the signs of the time will be terrifying things happening in the heavens. Jesus told us to look for these signs. Peter makes it very practical when he tells us, 'Because, my dear friends, you have a hope like this before you, I urge you to make certain that such a Day would find you at peace with God and man, clean and blameless in His sight' (2 Peter 3:13 PHILLIPS)."

We returned to the clubhouse and were seated again in our circle on the floor as the questions began to tumble out. It was an exciting time of sharing, and I was thankful for the shooting stars.

I told about the many signs that Jesus mentioned and that Luke 21:32 tells us that the generation that will see all these signs shall not pass away, until they are all fulfilled.

Jap was one of the girls who was a deep thinker. "I wonder, Tante Kees, if we are living in the generation when all the signs will be fulfilled and Christ will return. We should keep our triangle within the circle and not forget it!"

(The triangle represented the three stages of development: social, intellectual, and physical; the circle meant the spiritual development. We emphasized that when the triangle was within the circle, we were in the proper position in our lives as children of God.)

Milly was puzzled; this was only her second time in our club, and she was hearing us speak of spiritual matters that confused her. "What does that mean, about the triangle and the circle?" she said. "Are you speaking in a secret language?"

For the first time Mien spoke up. "It means . . . stop trying to work things out for yourself and ask God to do it. I tried hard, but it didn't help . . . now I have asked Him to manage me."

## On Parade

There was one outstanding yearly occasion when my father took a direct part in working with my girls. This was the important Holland holiday on the queen's birthday.

On August 31, Queen Wilhelmina's birthday, there was a great celebration, with parades and speeches, picnics and fairs. It was an old-fashioned Fourth of July done up in Dutch style. Father, as one of Haarlem's leading citizens, organized the activities of the day and sat on the platform with the mayor.

Since Father was the chairman of the parade committee, my Girl Guides always had a very prominent place in the lineup. We could display our flag, with the triangle inside the circle, and take that opportunity to explain to anyone who asked what the significance was of our symbol.

On one parade route we marched with an elaborate horsedrawn carriage, resplendent with liveried coachmen. It was so elegant that I couldn't resist poking my head out of the coach window and making a funny face. Father, however, was always dignified, in spite of his prankish daughter.

After Wilhelmina was replaced by her daughter, Juliana, as queen, the date for the celebration was changed to April 30. Since the following day was May Day, the occasion for the international communist parade, we always arranged for all the banners to be removed so that the communists couldn't take advantage of our decorations.

## Going International

The club work and Girl Guide activities grew each year, until some members of the YMCA in America heard of these efforts and invited me to an international conference in Riga, Latvia. Little Latvia was an independent country then, still able to practice religious freedom. After the communists seized Latvia in 1940, Christian practices were stamped out.

It was in the 1930s when I went to Latvia. On the way to the conference grounds, I was invited to be the guest of two old ladies in their home. Their country had been torn by wars and revolutions and had changed nationalities several times. During a revolution, the house of the old women had been raided, many of their valuable possessions were destroyed, including their antique wall clock. It had been repaired many times but never was able to strike the hours. The chain for the weight was hopelessly tangled, and I worked on the clock for quite some time, although I am a repairer of watches, not clocks. It was frustrating, so I talked over the problem with the Lord and He gave me the solution. I can still see the two ladies standing hand in hand, tears of joy on their faces, when they heard their clock strike again. That night, when one of them heard the clock, she awakened the other and whispered, "Father's clock is striking."

How glad I was that I was a watchmaker and could bring some happiness into their lonely lives.

At the conference I learned that I had a lot to learn! I heard about the leadership of Girl Guides in other countries and felt like a real beginner. The spiritual training, however, was a bit of a disappointment. There was a lot of talk about "character building," until finally I asked,

"Don't you think that we miss the purpose when we tell the girls to be good citizens but fail to bring them to Jesus Christ?"

To my amazement they changed the program because of that question. The talk about evangelization in the clubs had been planned for the last day, but it was rescheduled for the second day.

When I returned home, we decided to improve our image somewhat and have better uniforms. We made dark-blue uniforms, but if the girls didn't have enough money for that, we said that any navy-blue dress was adequate.

With my own homemade uniform, an orange ribbon substituted for the official Girl Guide's scarf, I went to my second international conference on a mountain near Vienna, Austria. There I met the top leaders of the Girl Guide movement in England, and they were very proper. Once we had an official roll call and I couldn't find my belt. I grabbed a belt from another dress and put that around my waist. We were making a horseshoe march in formation and a Dutch Girl Guide whispered to me in agony when she passed me, "You have two belts—one is hanging on your back."

Suddenly I felt very tacky; I compared my dress with the smart uniforms, perfect to the smallest detail. I began to feel like Alice in Wonderland when she grew into a giant. There I was with two belts and that glaring orange ribbon fastened to my front with a safety pin.

One of the Girl Guide officers said to me, "I'm glad that I had the chance to meet you and talk on top of this mountain, but if I meet you in such a uniform in London, I will act as if I have never seen you before."

After that experience I realized that this enterprise

was too serious to remain amateurish. When I returned to Holland, we asked some prominent and talented women to help us form a national board of directors. We studied handbooks from other areas and held many conferences. Since there were groups of women interested in this work from many different places in Holland, we chose a central meeting place—the railway station in Amsterdam. We could work in the quiet first-class waiting room until the moment our trains left.

But I became concerned about the direction of the Girl Guides. Coming in contact with leaders from other parts of the country, we discovered that "religious instruction" was not acceptable. It was considered propaganda for a religion. We could have clubs for Christian girls with Christian leaders, but our aim to reach the other girls was made impossible. It seemed that all the club work, Bible studies, conferences, camps were just preparation for something more. Consequently, a new Christian movement was born.

*De Nederlandse Meisjesclubs* (Netherlands Girls' Clubs) grew out of the Girl Guide movement but added the missing dimension. After a few years, the outreach of these clubs burst beyond the borders of Holland, and we had six thousand members in the Netherlands East Indies and eight hundred in the West Indies. Because of our symbol, the name of our club members was *Triangle Girls.*

The first article of our club law was impressed upon many young minds. It was: SEEK YOUR STRENGTH THROUGH PRAYER.

Years later, in a time when camping and parades, conferences and singing were beautiful memories of peaceful times, I was in a prison cell. Every sound was magnified in the deadly silence of those cubicles; I realized there was a girl crying next door. I called to her and said, "Don't cry, be strong . . . we'll be free soon."

The answer shocked me.

"Tante Kees . . . oh, Tante Kees . . . is that you? I'm Annie."

I recognized her voice. She was one of my faithful club girls, who had been arrested after my family and I had been taken to prison. My heart almost stopped. That poor girl was the last person I expected to be strong in such a terrible spot. I called to her through the barriers of the prison walls. "Annie, do you remember the first article of our club law? 'Seek your strength through prayer.'"

She stopped crying.

# 17

∞∞∞

# Opposition!

Opposition to lives that are yielded to Jesus Christ takes many forms, some dramatic, some subtle. Satan is a clever angel of light, but sometimes he chooses supernatural ways to frighten us into inactivity.

During a time at camp with the girls, I was singing outside of the cabin after lights-out. The song had the words: "Don't be afraid for whatever is coming, your heavenly Father takes care of you."

Suddenly I heard horrible noises around me. It seemed as if among the trees some sort of beings were trying to make me stop. The noises grew and subsided, sending shivers through my body with their weird tones. While I sang, I pleaded with the Lord: "Cover me and protect me with Your blood, Lord Jesus . . . give me the strength to go on singing and speak through me to reach all these girls."

The noises remained and got louder and more ugly, but I didn't stop. I knew that I stood on the front line of battle, but through Jesus, it was victory ground, not defeat or retreat. As soon as I had finished the song, the noises stopped, just as abruptly as they began.

I went to bed and thanked the Lord for His victory. The next morning I asked the girls if they had heard anything unusual the previous night. They answered that they had never heard me sing so beautifully. Nobody heard anything else.

## He Never Fails

Many of the girls in the clubs stand out in my memory. Peggy, for instance, was a member of the gym club who was not able to pay her dues, although it was only a *dubbeltje* (two cents). Unfortunately, we found that she stole from the club money, which was kept in a small box on the windowsill at the clubhouse. I was concerned about Peggy, so I marked a quarter and left it on the windowsill. When it disappeared, I called Peggy aside and asked to see her purse. There was the marked quarter.

Peggy had accepted the Lord as her Savior, but she was still bound to her past and background—a family of so-called down-and-outers. I told her, "Peggy, a child of God is tempted, but the difference from those who are not Christians is that God gives with the temptation a way of escape. He says, 'Confess your sins, God is faithful and just to forgive. . . .'"

Peggy understood and right then confessed what she had done. From that time on, we elected her treasurer of our club and there was never a cent lost. Peggy really meant business when she gave her yes to Jesus; she trusted Him, and I did too—that is why I could trust her. She never failed because Jesus never failed.

## The Only Comfort

Pietje was a hunchback, one of our best-liked club girls. Although it was a long time ago, I remember her reactions to the Bible stories. One day we were discussing Exodus 20:5, where God speaks to the Jewish people about the sins of the fathers continuing upon the children, grandchildren, and great-grandchildren. Pietje began to cry, and when I noticed her, I took her into another room to talk over her troubles.

Pietje's face was very dark as she said, "I am a hunchback and that was the punishment for my father who has been an alcoholic."

"But Pietje, did you hear the following verse: 'And showing mercy unto thousands of them that love me, and keep my commandments'? When your father begins to love God he will experience His mercy. You love the Lord, and although you are a hunchback, you are a happy girl, because you experience the mercy and peace in your heart because Jesus lives in you."

When Pietje was in a Bible study group we read Romans 8:34 and I asked, "Who is our Judge?" They answered, "Jesus!" and I said, "Who is our Advocate?" The answer came from Pietje, "Jesus!" Then she almost shouted, "What a joy! Judge and Advocate is the same! Jesus prays for us, so there is nothing to fear."

One day they sent for me to come quickly because Pietje was in a large ward of a hospital, and they told me she was dying. I knew that she had accepted Jesus as her Savior. As I stood beside her bed I said, "It's such a comfort to know Jesus is our Judge, also our Advocate. How He loves you!"

At that moment I saw the transformation on her face from pain to peace. "Pietje, can you hear me?" I said.

She didn't open her eyes. I couldn't reach her anymore; I prayed with her, laying my hand on her feverish head and asking the Good Shepherd to take His lamb in His arms and carry her straight through the valley of the shadow of death into the house of the Father with many mansions.

When I said, "Amen," Pietje opened her eyes for the last time and smiled.

Pietje was still very fresh in my mind and heart when I met the next day with leaders and board members of the YWCA. We talked about club experiences, and then one lady said, "I don't like the method of your clubs in Haarlem. All that preaching you do! I don't think it's right. I believe in Christian surroundings and bringing girls into a Christian atmosphere—that will attract far more girls than just Bible talks will. I preach by my behavior rather than by what I say."

My answer was, "Romans 10:14 says, 'How will they believe in Him whom they have not heard? And how will they hear without a preacher?'"

I'm glad that we told Pietje about our Judge and Advocate Jesus in the time we could still reach her. In the twenty-five years that we did club work, there were at least forty girls who died. Accidents, illnesses, even a murder were the causes. When I stood at the deathbed of a club girl, I was so thankful that I had redeemed the time when she was still able to listen to the gospel. Illness, pain, even drugs during the last part of a person's life may make it impossible for him to hear.

When Pietje died, I was the speaker at her burial. Father had conducted so many burial services for his colleagues that he was able to help me in so many ways. His straightforward testimony was not always appreciated, but when death entered a family, Father was a welcome comforter. When someone dies, people are confronted with eternity and there is the right opportunity to speak about the security of eternal life that only Jesus can give.

Father gave me some practical advice for those sad occasions: "When your time comes to speak, Corrie, don't hesitate. Many people are moved and nervous, so look for a place where everyone can hear and see you. Step forward without hesitation. Relatives and friends who are left behind must be challenged to repent of their sins and receive Jesus as their Savior."

Yes, opposition comes in strange places and through unusual vehicles: supernatural sounds from the darkness of a forest and even superficial attitudes from the self-righteous.

## Doubt

Opposition also came from within. Has there been doubt in my heart? Has there been dryness in my prayer life? Yes, indeed, there has been.

There was a time when I needed a major operation. For some strange reason, I persuaded the surgeon not to give me a general anesthetic, only a local. I didn't realize that this could be such a severe shock to my system. I didn't suffer pain during the operation, but I did have a great deal of tension. For several months afterward I needed some painful treatments.

In that time my mind and spirit were very low; I couldn't pray; the Bible was uninteresting; church was dull. I remember that my prayers were very short. Most of the time I muttered, "Lord, I can't reach You . . . I can't pray. Lord, I know that You can reach me. Keep me in Your care and help me to be able to pray again soon."

The outward Corrie was the same. I did the club work as I had always done. I worked in the shop, met customers, and carried on all the activities of our busy lives. I don't know if anyone saw what a dark valley I was going through, for I held it inside. I didn't talk over my problems with my family and friends. After all, I thought, they have worries enough. Now I know how stupid that was.

Then a girl, Colly, came to me and asked if she could tell me her troubles. She was a bright girl from a good, hardworking family, and I liked her very much.

"Tante Kees," she said with her head down, "can you help me? For weeks I have been unable to pray. Do you think I'm lost? Do you think I'm no longer a child of God?"

"Colly, you're a child of God and you're not lost. Now sit down and I'll tell you something about myself. I know exactly how you feel, because I'm going through the same problem as you. For several weeks I haven't been able to pray . . . but even though the time has been dark, I know that Jesus is with me and He can reach me. Let's see if there is something in the Bible that can help both of us."

We read Romans 8:26: "The Spirit also helps our weakness; for we do not know how to pray as we should, but the Spirit Himself intercedes for us."

Colly and I both realized that the Holy Spirit helps us with our daily problems and in our prayer problems. When we are totally inadequate, the Spirit is interceding with God the Father for us. The burden of guilt was taken from Colly and me, and together we thanked the Lord that He had forgiven us and restored our communication with Him.

## *Haarlemsche Meisjesclubs*

The H.M.C. (Haarlem Girls' Clubs) had a performance once each year in the concert hall, when each club demonstrated some of its skills and abilities. We opened the program with all of the 250 to three hundred girls marching onto the platform. They sang a song, and I gave a five-minute talk to the people in the auditorium.

The mixed club (which had passed the "year's trial" without any serious mishaps) provided the orchestra for the musical part of our entertainment. The first time this group had to play before all of those friends and relatives (about a thousand of them), they were frozen with stage fright. I walked over and picked up a violin and acted as if I were a real virtuoso, but making sure that no one in the audience saw that the bow was turned upside down and not touching the strings. As I "played" the violin, the boys gained confidence and began to perform. The ones who were playing wind instruments probably had trouble stifling their laughter in order to make music.

Tears and laughter, opposition and support—the clubs taught those young men and women preparation for life.

When the war started, we had to close the H.M.C. clubs. I will never forget the evening we were together for the last time. We saluted our flag, with tears running down our cheeks, and then folded it carefully and hid it in a secret closet of the clubhouse.

As we sang the national hymn for the last time together, the girls had a very difficult time. "Girls, we mustn't cry," I said. "We had great fun in the clubs, but it wasn't just for a good time that we have come together.

We have learned the important facts of what makes us strong, even in times of disaster. The Lord Jesus gives us security even in the insecurity of wartime."

I looked at those girls and wondered—would they draw on the Lord's strength in the days and years to come? What was in store for them in this world of ours that is filled with hatred and cruelty?

I was so grateful that the time in our clubs had not been wasted in just building "good citizens," but that we had the opportunity to learn the vital message of Jesus' victory, which would give strength for the suffering that awaited many of us.

# 18

## "... He Took My Hand"

War. It was early in the morning when we heard the bombs. We knew the sound of the explosions were coming from Schiphol, the airport near Haarlem. I ran to Betsie's room and found her sitting up in bed, pale and shaking. We put our arms around each other and trembled with each blast; the wavering red glow was so eerie in the darkness of our once-peaceful skies.

We were afraid but had learned from childhood how to cast our burdens on the Lord. We prayed like frightened children, running to their father for help and protection.

"Lord, make us strong . . . give us strength to help others."

"Lord, take away our fear. Give us trust."

It was a crisis of fear in both of us, but Jesus gave us the victory over it. We were never so frightened as we were during that night, not even when war and occupation destroyed our whole family life and everything we had known for more than a half a century. Was that night the Lord's way of inoculating us in preparation for the future?

In the five days of war that followed, many people came to the house; Father was a pillar of strength for all of them; he prayed with everyone who asked. Sometimes the shock of what was happening would engulf me, and while Father was bringing trust and peace to those in turmoil, I would go to the piano and play Bach. No other music gave me so much rest.

The darkest time during those five days was when our royal family left, our Queen Wilhelmina for England and Crown Princess Juliana for Canada. We knew then that our case was hopeless.

There were not many times that I cried, but when I heard about the royal family leaving the country, I was heartbroken and wept. For the Dutch people, the queen was our security—we loved her.

Then Holland surrendered. I walked in the street with Father, and everyone was talking to everyone else. In that moment there was a oneness that I have never seen before. We were together in the great suffering, humiliation, and defeat of our nation. Although my heart was aching with misery there was encouragement that people could be so united.

In the millennium we will be like that: The whole world will be covered with the knowledge of God like the waters cover the bottom of the sea. The oneness will not be in misery but in our communion with the Lord.

The German army marched through the Barteljorisstraat: tanks, cannons, cavalry, and hundreds and hundreds of soldiers. The narrow little street where Dot and I had played games, the alley where I had seen the drunks when I was only five and prayed for "all the people in the Smedestraat," the path we had taken on Sunday to St. Bavo's—all were filled with soldiers.

As the conquerors swept in, I noticed some of them

were red-faced, shame written in their expressions. After the war a German told me, "With every step I took in Holland, I felt ashamed. I knew I was occupying a neutral nation."

Churches were packed in those days; the psalms, which were written in times of great suffering, gained a new value. Ministers who had never preached about the second coming of Christ now chose their texts from the many places in the Bible on that subject.

In the beginning, we saw little change in our daily life, but gradually the enemy began to impose restrictions. At first the curfew was ten o'clock, which was not difficult for us, but later it was moved back to eight, then six. No one could leave his house; there was absolute blackout, and every window was covered with black paper as soon as the sun was down.

Telephones were cut off; food was rationed; and often after standing in long lines with our ration cards, we would find that the stores were empty.

One beautiful Sunday afternoon, Betsie, Father, and I were walking through our park, south of Haarlem, when the Gestapo descended and took all of the young fathers around us, who were out walking with their families, leaving distraught wives and crying children behind.

All Dutch people have bicycles, and sometimes the Gestapo set up a bicycle blockade. Everyone who rode by was summoned to give up his vehicle. If you were fortunate enough to keep your bicycle, you learned to ride without tires, because they were confiscated and taken to Germany.

We were not even safe in church. Once during a service in the cathedral, the Germans guarded the doors so that nobody could move. Then they opened one door and ordered every man from eighteen to forty to come out. They were sent that same day to Germany—many of these men were never seen again.

The occupation—the underground movement to save Jews—the concentration camps—all of these are documented in *A Prisoner and Yet . . .*, and in my book and the movie *The Hiding Place.*

For more than thirty years since World War II, I have been a tramp for the Lord in more than sixty countries on all the continents of this troubled world. Many people have asked me about my childhood, youth, and the years before *The Hiding Place.* A person doesn't spring into existence at the age of fifty; there are years of preparation, years of experience, which God uses in ways we may never know until we meet Him face to face.

However, from the perspective of over eighty years of living, I have had the marvelous opportunity to discover the sweetness of some of the fruit of His labor. Just recently I have heard from by letter or met in person some of my club "girls." (They are still girls to me!) It has been like a letter from the Lord.

### Aukje

One of our faithful club girls was quiet Aukje. She was a peacemaker who could say a few words but make them count. When other girls were unruly and stubborn, I remember Aukje saying, "Don't be so stupid. Why did we come to the club in the first place? Most of us want to have fun and learn something, so if you don't like it then leave and let the rest of us enjoy the club."

To the point—but said with such kindness that most of the time the problems were overcome. When she was about seventeen, Aukje became a club leader herself and led a group of girls who learned handcrafts. She was so quiet and gentle that we didn't expect exciting results from her, but her love for the Lord was very clear.

When the ten Boom family was arrested Aukje came to our house, not knowing that it was a Gestapo trap. She was taken to the police station and spent a week with our oldest Jewish underground girl, Mary, who had been in the hiding place but was later arrested in the street.

Aukje talked to Mary about the Lord Jesus. She told her that Jesus had died on the cross for the sins of the whole world and that He had said, "Come to Me, all who are heavy laden, I will give you rest."

Mary said, "I heard Grandpa ten Boom pray so often when I was in the Beje. He always said to me, 'Mary, you are a Jew; you will not change that if you invite the Lord Jesus into your heart. On His divine side He was the Son of God, but on His human side He was a Jew.'"

Mary received Jesus as her Savior in that cell. Our quiet Aukje had a boldness for the Lord. She told me later that the moment Mary said her yes to Jesus in her prayer of accepting Him, the guards came into the cell and took her away. We heard later that she was sent to Poland where she died.

I heard nothing from Aukje for many years. What a surprise it was for me when she came to my room in Haarlem thirty years later. She told me that she was working in a small village where there was no minister; she preaches every Sunday for the little congregation. She said, "What I learned in your clubs I still use when I teach the children and have my Bible study groups."

## Poes

Poes was an outgoing little rascal; wherever she was in a club there was laughing and fun. At camp she was the happy note, even when it was raining and attitudes were down. When there were weaker girls who needed help in hikes or gymnastics, Poes was always ready to help.

I remember one time she was walking behind me and was quite outspoken in her ideas about my legs. She said, "If I had such legs, I should decide to march beside them." She married an older boy and moved to South Africa. I met them there once after the war, but only briefly. He called himself an atheist but did not object when Poes and I shared with him our love for the Lord Jesus. I promised to pray for him, but in later correspondence Poes never mentioned that he was interested in spiritual affairs.

Then a strange thing happened—one of those "coincidents," which are such a marvelous part of God's plan. Poes and her husband were walking in the streets of Johannesburg when a boy asked them to buy a raffle ticket to raise money for a house for a boys' club. Poes said, "Sure, I enjoyed clubs when I was a girl—I hope you have a lot of fun in your new cabin."

Later she found out that they had the ticket that won the first prize in the raffle—it was a round-trip plane ride for two to the Netherlands! And so it happened that one day they stood in my room in Holland. What memories we shared! Poes told me she had become a member of a church, and Henk, her husband, listened with amusement as we talked about the clubs. He declared very strongly that he didn't believe in God. I knew I had only one chance to bring him the gospel, so I said, "Henk, I'll probably only have this one time to talk with you. There are two ways to live: You can go your way or God's way; you can accept Jesus Christ as your Savior, and He will make you a child of God. Then you can bring Him all your sins and ask and get forgiveness. He makes sure you're a child of God, and He will put your name in the book of life."

After I prayed with them, Henk said, "I believe it's time that I gave my heart to Jesus. I've seen much of Him in the life of Poes, and He must be a reality. I know I'm a sinner and you said that Jesus accepts sinners. So I'll tell Him all that I have done and I have been, and believe that He will make me a child of God."

They returned to South Africa, and Henk became a member of a lively church. Some months ago Henk died, but he said, "Tell Tante Kees that God has used her to bring me to the Lord."

God began working years before in a mischievous little girl, Poes, in a gymnastics club in a little Dutch town.

### The Golden Tea Party

What would they be like? Would the years have changed them? What joys and sorrows, trials and triumphs would they have seen in the decades since we had last met?

I was so excited, as that younger Corrie had been when she introduced her club girls at the yearly performance in the Haarlem concert hall. Now in my eighties, I had returned to Holland for a visit and had invited those women who had been in clubs in years past—and were still in the vicinity of Haarlem—to my house for tea.

No uniform with two belts and a safety pin this time!

I wore my best red and white silk summer dress and made sure that not one thing would mar my appearance.

They arrived at the front door at the same time. Some came on their big old-fashioned bicycles, some drove little cars, and others walked from the bus stop. There was no need for protocol, for they began to laugh and talk all at once.

What an afternoon we had! Each girl told a little of her story, ending on the same theme, which added so much joy to my heart.

Ariapja, whose nickname was *Jap*, bubbled with her enthusiasm about the club work. She told how she first became a part of our group and her mother had said, "You may not have a uniform!"

So she went to her first camp feeling a bit ashamed, because she wasn't dressed like the rest of the girls. It was the most important issue in her life then. Hank, who had also come for tea that afternoon, was the one who gave Jap her uniform; that unselfish act was remembered by Jap all her life. When she went home she asked her mother if she could be a Girl Guide. Her mother told her that it was all right, if she didn't wear the uniform on Sunday.

Girl guiding became Jap's life, and she told us that sunny afternoon in my living room in Holland that much she learned as a young girl in the clubs had prepared her for her total life experiences.

Stien had gone to one of my clubs when she was sixteen to learn the catechism. I had been her teacher, and after she was received into the Dutch Reformed church I said, "Now, Stien, you must lead a club."

After Stien had been one of our club leaders, she took the initiative and began a club for feebleminded children.

She told me later, "You had taught me, Tante Kees, to love those less fortunate, and I truly did love those children." For Stien going to the clubs was the best part of her young life. Her home was never open to others, and she spent many evenings at the Beje. Fortunately, she had stayed at home on that fateful day in February 1944 when the Gestapo paid us an unwelcome visit.

Annie, who had answered a newspaper advertisement to join a club, said that she came for fun and not for all those "spiritual things." And she did have fun! She joined the singing club, the English club, and the gymnastics club, and when she told about the latter, she reminded all of us about the club slogan. (I knew someone would bring that up—the rascals!) The gymnastics club slogan—WE MAKE STRAIGHT WHAT IS CROOKED—was not very good— too long to put on a program. (I had to pretend not to notice the laughter every time it was mentioned.)

Annie told how she fell in love with the gym teacher. However, when his girlfriend came, Annie became very jealous and out of spite sewed his pants together and put water in his shoes.

(Tea cups almost fell off laps when this story was recounted.)

As a punishment, I told Annie that she would not be allowed to go to the club for three weeks. She reminded me, however, that she returned in one week, proving that Tante Kees's discipline was sometimes a little lax.

When Annie was seventeen, she was at the camp at Bliscap, feeling very low. She had just split up with her current boyfriend and thought it was the end of the world. She remembered that we were sitting outside looking at the stars and I had told her, "When you're in need and don't know the answer, tell the Lord about it. He has your past, present, and future in His hands." It was then that Annie accepted Jesus Christ as her Savior; she said that every time she was in need in years to come she remembered that moment.

"I know the Lord is willing to take your life in His hands when you're small," Annie said.

Nellie was born in Germany and didn't come to Holland until she was fourteen years old. She came into the clubs when she was eighteen, not as a believer in Jesus Christ, but found Him during one of the camps. When Nellie remembered the outstanding experiences of her club time, she talked about the campfires—the time of deep discussions together. She thought a while when we asked what club work had prepared her for. Then she remembered one of the articles in the club law, which was to give help to others. She said that even today people know there is help in her home. "Let's go over to Nell's— she always has the soup on."

As the girls began to share more and more of their memories and their later life experiences, one story after another spilled out. Reina told how she loved the circle and the club song. It was difficult for Ellen de Kroon, my secretary, and Carole Carlson to contain themselves as we all stood up and joined hands to repeat our motto and sing our song after almost forty years of separation! The voices may have changed a bit, but the fervor was still there!

Reina said she had come from a Christian family, but the club work had inspired in her the personal desire to bring the gospel to other girls.

"Did you know," she said, looking around the room, "that the last time the Girl Guides wore their uniforms was at my wedding?"

Hank was in at the start of the clubs and remembered

the first camp experience she had. One of the girls had trouble with sleepwalking, and she told how Tante Kees had been so concerned about her and had walked her gently back to bed. However, it was also discovered that the so-called sleepwalker had a sweet tooth, for the following morning the chocolate bars, which had been left out for campfire treats, had been strangely consumed by someone in her sleep.

Julie had been rather quiet but finally began to bring the conversation back to the present. "I want so much to give our young people some of the love, the experiences, the strength in knowing the Lord that we learned in your clubs, Tante Kees. Our children have so much—and yet they're so poor. They're so free today—much more so than we were—and yet they face many more dangers from the world."

It became very still in the room. Everyone had her own thoughts about children, grandchildren—our youth, who face the "wars and rumors of wars" that exist in a world racing toward self-destruction.

I looked through my small living room into the dining room, where Papa's portrait hangs. I could see him at the oval table, head bowed, praying: "Lord, bless the queen; we thank You for this beautiful Lord's Day and for the promise of Your soon coming. Thank You for this food and for this family. In the name of Jesus Christ, Amen."

How grateful I am to have lived in my Father's house! Yes, Lord, I thank You for this family. I looked at my friends, gathered for an afternoon of tea and memories, and thanked the Lord for the family of believers all over this globe. How the love of God stretched in and out of the watchmaker's shop to all parts of the world—to mansions in California and hospitals in Kenya, from queens to prison guards.

As the "golden tea party" ended and the club girls left, we broke some of our Dutch restraint and hugged each other. Many of them had suffered much through the years, and yet they had remained strong in the Lord. I realized that all we do through our own strength has to be cleansed, but what we do through the Lord has value for time and eternity.

This is no time to look back. What challenges we have today! I remember what Father often said: "When Jesus takes your hand He keeps you tight. When Jesus keeps you tight He leads you through life. When Jesus leads you through life, He brings you safely home."

# Amazing Love

Corrie ten Boom

**Guideposts**®

CARMEL, NEW YORK 10512

www.guidepostsbooks.com

This Guideposts edition is published by special arrangement with
Revell, a division of Baker Book House Company.

© 1953 by Corrie ten Boom

Published by Fleming H. Revell
a division of Baker Book House Company
P.O. Box 6287, Grand Rapids, MI 49516-6287

Previously published in 1953 by Christian Literature Crusade
and in 1964 by Fleming H. Revell.

Printed in the United States of America

*Library of Congress Cataloging-in-Publication Data*
Ten Boom, Corrie.
    Amazing love / Corrie ten Boom.
        p.      cm.—(Corrie ten Boom library)
    Originally published: Christian Literature Crusade, 1953.
    ISBN 0-8007-1766-X (cloth)
    1. Ten Boom, Corrie. 2. Christian biography—Netherlands.
    I. Title. II. Series.
    BR1725.T35A3      1999
    269'.2'092—dc21                                         98-48309

Scripture quotations are from the King James Version of the Bible.

For current information about all releases from Baker Book House, visit our Web site:
www.bakerbooks.com

Interior design by Holly Johnson
Front cover design by Cathy Kovacs/Enterprise Four
Back cover design by Dennis Arnold
Typeset by Composition Technologies, Inc.

# Contents

## Contents

# Foreword

"Ye shall be witnesses unto Me," said Jesus to His disciples, "unto the uttermost part of the earth." Corrie ten Boom is one of that number. Having found for herself the victory that overcomes the world in the horrors of a concentration camp, she cannot keep her secret to herself. She has become a worldwide witness, a troubadour of Christ. She shares with us in these pages, with all the vividness of firsthand experience, contacts and conversations with all sorts in camps and jails, with actresses and students, with the sophisticated and illiterate. And I lay down this manuscript saying, like those two disciples of old, "Did not our heart burn within us, while He talked with us by the way?" For I met, not Corrie, but Corrie's Christ. I was blessed again and again by the instances of her own childlike dependence on Him as her wisdom, by His responses to her faith, and by the wise and winning ways in which she has been able to commend Him to so many. May many who read these living chapters see Him again in the simplicity of faith as our all-sufficiency and be stirred as I have been to a bolder faith.

*Norman P. Grubb*

## 1

## *P*lans

Human hearts are amazingly alike.

The silence of night had fallen on seven hundred women, lying tightly packed together, asleep in the barracks of a concentration camp.

Bep, my sister, awakened me and repeated to me in a whisper what God had told her about the work that would be waiting for us after our release.

"We must open a home for people who have suffered so much here and in other places where life has been completely disrupted by war. But the most important part of our task will be to tell everyone who will listen that Jesus is the only answer to the problems that are disturbing the hearts of men and of nations. We shall have the right to speak because we can tell from our experience that His light is more powerful than the deepest darkness. Surely, nothing could be darker than our experiences here. I keep telling myself, 'things cannot possibly grow worse,' but every day we see that misery only deepens. How wonderful that the reality of His presence is greater than the reality of the hell about us! We shall have to do a lot of traveling, but we must never spend our energies in collecting funds. God will provide everything we need:

money, health, wisdom, and the necessary languages. All of our efforts must go into bringing the gospel, for we shall have many opportunities."

Bep's eyes did not see the dirty throng around us. She was gazing into the future, and a glow of happiness brightened her emaciated face.

Three days later she passed away, and ten days later, just one week before all women of my age were killed, I was released from the concentration camp.

In this book I shall describe some of my experiences during the first years of my wanderings. Why should I do this? Because I have discovered that there are many people who need this message.

Human hearts are amazingly alike. As I talk with people in America, England, Switzerland, Germany, and Holland, I frequently find the same need, the same ignorance of what we can be in Jesus Christ, if only we accept the Bible in a simple, childlike way as the Word of God, the Word that teaches us the foolishness of God that is wiser than the wisdom of men, the love of God that passes all understanding.

When we read the Bible we should never use as our guide the wisdom of men or the standards of our own reason.

I was once a passenger aboard a ship that was being guided by radar. The fog was so dense we couldn't see even the water about us. But the radar screen showed a streak of light, indicating the presence of another ship far ahead. The radar penetrated the fog and picked up its image. So, also, is faith the radar that sees reality through the clouds.

The reality of the victory of Christ can be seen only by faith, which is our radar. Our faith perceives what is actual and real; our senses perceive only that which is limited to three dimensions and comprehended by our intellect. Faith sees more.

I am not a scholar, but much of the little I do know I learned as I faced death in front of the crematorium in Ravensbrück. That is why God sometimes uses me to help people who know far more than I.

2

*Forgiveness*

And when ye stand praying, forgive, if ye have ought against any: that your Father also which is in heaven may forgive you your trespasses.

*Mark 11:25*

Why should we hold on to the sins of others while our own sins have been cast into the depths of the sea?

I was a guest on one of the farms on the vast prairies of Kansas. How far the horizons stretch out on every hand! And how clear the air! We Hollanders are accustomed to a shading of color and line in our landscape, due to the atmosphere. But here everything is clearly visible at three hundred yards or more, and seems close by. When the sun sets, the shadows fall stark and clear from barn, cows, and even the tasseled corn.

The family with which I was staying was a large one, and I always have an especially good time when I am taken right into the life of a typical American family. The youngest daughter here was just finishing high school, and all of us planned to attend the graduation exercises the following week.

All of us? Something was threatening to mar the joy of

that happy occasion. For months past there had been dissension between the father and his eldest son. In a fit of anger, the father had shown his son the door and forbidden him ever to cross its threshold again. The mother told me the whole story in confidence. For her the graduation festivities would be no joy. "My boy has a farm not far from here," said she, "but I'm sure he will not want to come."

We prayed together about it, and then I waited for the opportunity I knew God would prepare for me.

I was having quite a few interesting experiences on the farm. I had helped drive the tractor, and, although the farmer stood behind me, I was still proud of having finished the corners so neatly.

One afternoon I went riding. The whole family stood watching as I mounted. The horse was being difficult, and, ignoring the reins entirely, walked over to the watering trough, began to drink, and then put his feet into the trough. I had all I could do to keep from pitching forward over his head. Finally, with the efforts of all, the horse was led to the road; but I had to take a lot of bantering advice and laughter about my first riding lesson. Once on the road, however, everything was fine. The horse was walking quietly now. The whole prairie lay stretched out before me. I inhaled deeply the pure air. The corn rustled and the wind played with my hair.

What a delight it is to look out over the world from the back of a horse!

Then the farmer rode up alongside of me, and before I knew it, there it was, the opportunity for which we had prayed.

"Have you ever prayed 'forgive us our debts as we for-give our debtors'?" I asked him. "Do you know what has become of your sins? If you believe in Jesus Christ and belong to Him, they have been cast into the depths of the sea, and that's very deep. But then He expects also that you will forgive the sins of your boy and cast them into the depths of the sea. Just imagine how you would feel if there should be another war, if your son had to go back into service and was killed in action. Don't you think you should forgive him right now? The love that God has for you in Christ Jesus is the same love that He will pour out into your heart through His spirit. If you open your heart to receive it, then His love will become your love, and His forgiveness your forgiveness."

All through the conversation I continued praying that the demon of bitterness would not win the conflict going on in the heart of the farmer.

After we had been riding for some time in silence, he said suddenly, "I'm going to see my son tonight. Will you go with me?"

And so we did. The old man was a bit uncomfortable as he stepped into the house. The son looked up in sur-prise. Then the father put his hand on the shoulder of the young man and said—was I hearing correctly?—"My boy, will you forgive me?"

I turned and walked quickly around to the other side of the house, but I could still hear the son's reply, "But, Father, I should ask you for forgiveness."

The graduation party was a great success.

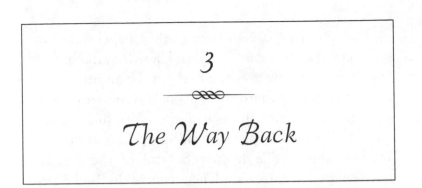

*3*

## The Way Back

Yesterday is a canceled check.
Today is cash.
Tomorrow is a promissory note to them that accept
the victory of Jesus.

Years ago when my father was assisting in the rehabilitation of prisoners, he asked me if I would like to help him and become a regular visitor to prison cells. I answered, "Please, Father, don't ask me to do anything like that. I wouldn't dare even enter a prison, to say nothing of going into the cells." But now that I myself have been a prisoner this fear is completely gone, and I try whenever possible to preach the gospel in prisons.

I had received an invitation to visit Sing Sing and was now about to see this modern penal institution.

In the parking lot were the cars of a visiting football team that had come to match its skill with the Sing Sing eleven. Several gates were opened and closed behind us, and then we were driven in a real prison van up the high hill on top of which the buildings are located. I couldn't help thinking of the van in which I had been taken to the prison at Scheveningen. Other than this, however, there was no similarity, for this did not look much like a prison.

On an open space in front of the chapel were many prisoners walking about freely, and here they did not wear uniforms. The view over the river was beautiful.

In the chapel there were about a hundred prisoners and only one guard. It looked like an ordinary church service. The men sang with enthusiasm, and one after another suggested a hymn. (Several of the prisoners were taking a correspondence course in Bible study at Moody Bible Institute.) There was an "openness" that made it easy for me to speak. My text was "For we wrestle not against flesh and blood, but against principalities . . . against spiritual wickedness in high places" (Ephesians 6:12).

I told the men how, in Ravensbrück, where I so often saw death about me, I had suddenly realized that life is, after all, very simple, but that it is we who make it involved. The devil is more powerful than we are, but Jesus is more powerful than the devil. Now if we belong to Jesus, we are on the victorious side. He came to destroy the works of the devil. We are not only striving toward victory but fighting from the position of victory.

After the service several of the prisoners came to shake hands with me. With one of them I had a long talk, and finally he said, "For a long time I have been unable to find the way back. Now I know—Jesus is the way."

# 4

——— ∞ ———

# *An Unexpected Feast*

On Calvary two malefactors were crucified: Which of them is you?

In the smaller towns and villages of the United States, the sheriff's house often also serves as a jail. It was on a Sunday afternoon that we rang the bell of such a home and asked if I could speak to the prisoners.

"Go right ahead," said the sheriff. "We haven't many customers right now, but if you think it worthwhile I'll be glad to take you to them."

It was a wretched little jail. Along one side of the cells were barred doors standing open. A narrow passage in front of the cells was also barred, and beyond these bars were some small windows. There were only three prisoners, a man and two boys.

Right here, I had one of those rare spiritual feasts that can come to one so unexpectedly in life. In the narrow passage in front of the cells I sat down and began to talk, my Bible open on my knees. The man was sitting on a stool at a small table. One of the boys sat on the floor with his legs crossed and his back against the bars. The other boy stood leaning against the door of his dirty cell.

After I had told them about the victory of Christ over sin, the man began to speak. He told his story of drunkenness and crime, and then turned to the boy beside him.

"What she said is true. It's only since coming here to serve my term that I've done what she advises. I've said yes to Jesus. And it isn't as hard as I thought it would be. You know what she said about faith being like that radar apparatus through which you could see a ship coming right through the fog? That's exactly the way it is. I have always seen only the clouds and fog and have never understood that the ship might be there. Now, suddenly, I see Him, right through everything. Jesus is a reality. He loves you so much that if you were the only human being on earth He would still have thought it worthwhile to die for you on the cross."

"I've never had a single person who cared anything about me," said the boy.

"Then you've found your Man now. For God so loved the world that He gave His only begotten Son, that whosoever—and that means you too—believeth on Him should not perish, but have everlasting life."

That afternoon both boys surrendered their lives to Christ.

# 5

## Be Not Afraid

Do not ask "What can I do?" but "What can He not do?"

Things do not always work out as smoothly as they did in the home of the sheriff.

One day I was permitted to join a "team" that worked regularly in a large prison. It was a most unusual building. We set our portable organ down in a long, narrow corridor barred at both ends. Only three faces were visible behind the barred cells, both to the right and left of us. Evidently I would have to keep turning my head from one direction to the other while speaking.

One of the women opened the service by singing to the accompaniment of the organ. She sang in a very affected manner, and the response was anything but favorable. At both ends of the corridor the prisoners began shrieking, yelling, and screaming to drown the voice of the singer. But she went calmly on with her song. Mixed with it all I could hear scornful, jeering laughter. Then one of the young men with us began to pray, speaking in a very unctuous manner. The effect was even worse. The prisoners had found a pail and were rolling it back and forth over the floor. The din was terrific. "Lord, must I speak in this place? I cannot," I prayed in desperation.

"Be not afraid; only believe. You can do all things through Him who strengthens you. There will be a great victory," said the Lord to me.

Then I dared to start. The noise grew even worse. Benches were thrown to the floor. There was an infernal clamor from all sides. But I was no longer afraid. I had the promise of victory, and so I tried to shout above the din. I bellowed, "When I was alone in a cell for four months—"

Suddenly there was a dead silence. What? That lady alone in a cell for four months? Prisoners always feel very sorry for me when I tell them about this part of my life. To be in solitary confinement is a severe punishment everywhere in the world. Most prisoners have learned that from experience.

Above the heads of the three prisoners behind the bars appeared more faces. They brought benches and chairs and climbed up on them to see us better. More and more faces appeared at both ends of the corridor. It was deadly quiet now, and I talked and talked, for three quarters of an hour. There was joy in my heart. The love of God was there. God's Spirit was working, and when I had finished, and the minister who was with us asked the men to surrender their lives to Christ, there were six who said yes. The minister went to one end of the corridor and I to the other, each taking three of these men who had raised their hands, to speak to them further. Now I could see that there was a large room beyond the end of the corridor where many prisoners were gathered together. Evidently all the men had to listen to the service whether they wanted to hear the Word or not.

It was quiet as I spoke to the three men. Then I looked around and addressed them all.

"Never before have I heard such awful noise during a service as here when I first began to speak. I was so glad that you soon quieted down. But do you know what I'm a bit afraid of now? That you will tease these men who held up their hands, or laugh at them. Please don't do that. These three men have made their decision for Jesus Christ and are now standing on the side of victory. They have received a booklet called 'The Gospel According to St. John.' Let them read it to you now and then. I hope that some day you too will say yes to Christ. I know that it will make you happy."

# 6

---

# The Word of God Is Living
## and Powerful

"The sword of the spirit, which is the Word of God,"
is far more powerful than our own arguments.

We were sitting on the veranda of a university dormitory, and a Mrs. Jameson was commenting on the lecture I had given only a few moments before.

"What you just told the students was very interesting, but I do not think you are right. Please do not take it ill of me, but I have had a wider experience than you. I am a member of an association that has taken me all over the world, and I have talked with outstanding persons in India, Arabia, Japan, and many other countries. I have discussed the road of life through time and eternity with Mohammedans, Brahmins, Shintoists, and many others. There were excellent people among them who came to know God without Jesus Christ. You told the students so positively that we need Him, but that is not true."

"Your argument is not with me, but with the Bible," said I. "It is not I who say so, but the Bible. Jesus said, 'No man cometh unto the Father, but by Me'" (John 14:6).

I felt somewhat abashed. A sense of inadequacy often

comes over me when I talk with people who are so much better informed than I. At such times this work seems much too difficult for me. Later on I talked it over with a friend who said, "You should not try to be anything but an open channel for the Spirit of God. You never can be anything else, even though you may think so at times. Follow the pathway of obedience, and you will be used by God far beyond your own powers."

A reception was being held in Ottawa, Canada, for all who wished to meet Prince Bernhard of the Netherlands. It was a pleasure to see so many Hollanders together. The prince looked tired but was cheerful and kind to everyone who addressed him. Photographers surrounded him as they took pictures of him from all sides, in conversation with some important person, or with a sweet country child in his arms.

I met many old acquaintances. And then, suddenly, I was face to face with Mrs. Jameson.

"I am glad to see you," said she. "You know, I just cannot forget what you said to me when you spoke at our university. Jesus said, 'No man cometh unto the Father, but by Me'; I keep thinking about that."

"How wonderful!" I said. "You have listened to the voice of God. Now go on listening and read the Bible. He still has much more to say to you."

The Word of God is living and powerful.

# 7

## The Sea Is Deep

I know beyond the shadow of doubt
My debt of sin has been wiped out.

There was to be a dinner party in a beautiful home beside a river. Several students had also been invited. It was approximately a two-hour drive from the city, but the people of Georgia do not seem to consider that a great distance. My host and I drove out along roads bright with oleanders blooming on either side.

We arrived just in time to see a glorious sunset. The sky above the water was ablaze with blue and gold as we sat on the beautiful terrace among the palms and enjoyed the warm evening air.

Servants were moving quietly about serving refreshments. It seemed as if time itself moved more slowly here. No one was in a hurry, nor was the conversation superficial.

I had spoken the night before on the subject, "The problem of sin has been solved on the cross of Jesus Christ." And I was glad to see that Jack was present tonight, because I had seen a look of obvious distaste on his face during my talk the night before and had not had the opportunity of discussing it with him.

This is an example of my reason for feeling that there is a great disadvantage in not speaking more than once to the same group. The danger is that the work then becomes superficial. The friendly and even sincere words, "I enjoyed your message," are not the only result I want to attain. I want people to come to an understanding of who Jesus is and how He wants to be the renewer of our lives.

And now Jack said, "I believe that there is remission of sins through Jesus Christ, but redemption? No, I can't see that. You said yesterday, 'The blood of Jesus Christ cleanseth us from all sin.' You showed us your hand and illustrated the text by saying, 'This morning my hand was dirty. Where is the dirt now? I don't know; I washed my hands. And so, too, Jesus washes away our sins. He casts them into the depths of the sea. They are gone, as far as the east is removed from the west.' That may be your opinion, but I don't believe it. We have to carry the consequences of our sins as long as we live. I believe in the forgiveness of sins, yes, but not in redemption."

After dinner we continued our talk in the garden. There were only three of us now: John, with whom I had been working for the past two weeks, and Jack, who was relating his experiences to us. It can be such a release to unburden one's soul completely.

It was a sad story.

"We were not very good boys in high school. I dated a lot of different girls, and one time things went wrong. I had to marry the girl, and four months later the baby came. Nobody knows that I am married, and no one must find it out. I want to become a minister, but if people hear about this my whole career will be gone. I am living a lie and don't know what to do about it. I'll have to bear the consequences of my sin as long as I live. That is what I mean by 'forgiveness, yes, but no remission.'"

As he spoke I continued praying for wisdom. How could I explain to him the mystery of the renewal of life through the victory of Jesus Christ?

Then John began to speak.

"Nevertheless, there is redemption. Jesus does not patch things up. He renews. If you will ask Him to go back with you to that dark spot in your life, He will change its darkness into light. That was His purpose in coming to us. He delivered us from all sin.

"Jesus lifts you up out of the cycle of cause and effects into the realm of His wonderful love. And one of the products of that love is grace."

"What is grace?"

"It's what Isaiah meant when he said, 'Instead of the thorn shall come up the fir tree.' Instead of a curse there will be a blessing.

"'Instead of the brier shall come up the myrtle tree.' Instead of a sinner there will be a saint.

"In Christ we are, you and I, the righteousness of God. Don't you understand that?

"Of course you don't. We'll understand these things only when we get to heaven and have new minds and other means of perception. But even now we can understand these things by faith. If you will now accept in faith that Jesus is the victor over the past, present, and future of everyone who surrenders his life completely to Him, He will change that dark spot in your life into a blessing. Then you will always see in that woman and child a living symbol of the forgiveness and redemption of Jesus Christ."

"But what must I do?" asked Jack. "I have been converted, as people call it, and I have accepted Jesus as my personal Savior."

"You still have to surrender your life completely to Him. Turn over all the keys of your life to Him. To lose your life for His sake means to save it. In His great love He demands your complete surrender."

Jack looked around. We were alone in the garden. From the house came a hubbub of many voices.

"I am willing to do it, but I don't know how to express it," he said.

"Just ask the Spirit of God to give you the right words."

All three of us then prayed, and Jack said, "I don't understand these things, but here I am, Lord. I know that You have said, 'Him that cometh unto Me I will in no wise cast out,' and 'A broken and a contrite heart, O God, Thou wilt not despise.'"

Just then I was called into the house, for they expected me to speak again to the guests. An hour later as I was leaving, Jack said to me, "Corrie, I can laugh again; I haven't been able to laugh for a year. But now I am free."

And I knew that it was true.

I don't know what the results of his deliverance will be, but he will no longer have to live a lie. His life is in good hands.

"If the Son therefore shall make you free, ye shall be free indeed" (John 8:36). And Jack will be used to help many who are in despair because of the consequences of their sins.

Our sins in the depths of the sea!

How tremendously great is the remission and redemption of sins through Jesus Christ!

Many Christians do not sufficiently realize the work that Jesus Christ is doing for us at this very moment. Many of us believe that He died for our sins. We believe in His death and resurrection, but we forget that after His resurrection, He ascended into heaven and sat down on the right hand of the Father and began to live for us as truly as He died for us.

The devil makes accusations against us day and night. But Jesus is our advocate. In Him we are the righteousness of God (2 Corinthians 5:21).

If, after having been forgiven for a sin, we are still worrying about it, even for five minutes more, we are robbing both Him and ourselves of much joy.

"Resist the devil, and he will flee from you" (James 4:7). No better weapon could be found to use against him than this text.

The consciousness of sin may degenerate into defeatism, "It's too bad, but that's the way I am." The devil rejoices when we are defeated but is afraid of the consciousness of victory.

The devil makes us conscious of sin.

The spirit of God makes us conscious of sin, and then conscious of victory.

# 8

---ᨒ---

# Never Again to Germany

When Jesus tells us to love our enemies, He Himself will give us the love with which to do it. We are neither factories nor reservoirs of His love, only channels. When we understand that, all excuse for pride is eliminated.

Returning to Holland after my release from the German concentration camp at Ravensbrück, I said, "One thing I hope is that I'll never have to go to Germany again. I am willing to go wherever God may want me to go; but I hope He'll never send me to Germany."

If we want to experience the guidance of God in our lives, we must accept one condition: obedience to Him.

On my trips to the United States I often spoke on the conditions in Europe during the post-war years, and when I talked of the chaos in Germany, people sometimes asked me, "Why don't you go to Germany, since you know the language?"

But I didn't want to go.

Then darkness came into my fellowship with God; when I asked for His guidance, there was no answer.

Now God does not want us ever to be in doubt as to what His guidance is, and so I knew that something had come between God and me, and I prayed, "Lord, is there some disobedience in my life?"

The answer was very distinct: "Germany."

Before me I could see again the land I had left in 1944. In my mind I could hear the harsh voices, "Schneller, aber schneller" (faster, faster), and my answer to God was long in coming.

"Yes, Lord, I'll go to Germany too. I'll follow wherever You lead."

Then, when I returned to Holland from the United States, I learned that it was not yet possible for Hollanders to obtain a visa for visiting Germany.

And I was glad.

I received an invitation to attend an International Conference in Switzerland; and God told me that I would meet some Germans there who would help me obtain a visa. Arriving at the conference, I found representatives from many countries, but not one single German.

And I was glad.

But on the last day of the conference, there were two new arrivals. The instant they appeared, I could see they were German. I asked them if they could help me with my papers, and one of the latecomers turned out to be a director of the Evangelisches Hilfswerk, the church organization for the assistance of refugees.

"If I send you an invitation to come to Germany, you will be able to get your visa," he said.

And so I went back to Germany.

Was it difficult? At times it was, at times it was not.

There is a sanctified Germany and a poisoned Germany. There is a Germany that has lost everything, where the hearts of people are a vacuum. Who is going to fill them? It is wonderful to be able to speak there about Him who renews hearts and fills them with His joy.

Years ago, I told the story of Jesus feeding the five thousand with five loaves and two fishes to a class of feeble-minded boys. Carl had become so absorbed in the story that he jumped to his feet and shouted, "There is enough! There is enough! Take as much as you want; there is enough!"

Dear little Carl, I wish more people were as much on fire about it as you.

Here we have the great riches of the Bible, and people misuse their time quibbling about its interpretation.

Is this a time for controversy?

Just imagine that your house was on fire, and the firemen were wrangling about their uniforms.

I heard that General MacArthur asked for a thousand missionaries to preach the gospel in Japan. There is a hunger for the gospel in that country. The harvest is plenteous; the laborers are few.

Not only there.

Also in Germany.

# 9

## My Chocolate Sermon

Though Jesus in Bethlehem a thousand times were born, and not in my heart, I would still be forlorn.

I was again in a German concentration camp for women.

Wooden barracks in the heart of a beautiful forest.

The superintendent was a friendly German woman who tried to keep her charges under control in "the democratic manner": no jumping to attention, no bellowed commands, no interminable roll calls as in Ravensbrück. But still it was a concentration camp, and it was surrounded by a barbed-wire fence.

In the camp I encountered "Aufseherinnen," women guards from Ravensbrück, where I myself had been imprisoned. Now they were prisoners, and I was free, free to walk out that gate any time to the freedom of the life outside. They would have to stay. I had come here to show these people the way to real freedom. I had come to speak of the love of God that passes all understanding, to tell about Jesus Christ, who came into this world to make people happy under all circumstances.

But—it was not easy to reach through to these people. In one of the factory barracks they were sitting in front of me. Each one had brought a chair from her own dormitory barracks. Their faces were glum, and it seemed as if I were addressing a stone wall. I kept praying that the love of God would fill me and shine through me. But all I could see was aversion and bitterness.

All of the women had Bibles with them and were evidently very familiar with them, because they found the texts I cited without any difficulty.

After having spoken in this camp twice, I consulted the superintendent.

"Can you tell me why I get no response at all?"

She laughed and answered, "The women have said to me, 'This Dutch woman speaks in such a simple way. We Germans are more highly cultivated and so much more profound in our theology.' I'm afraid you won't get along too well together. But why don't you try once more. You have permission to speak three times."

When I got home, I went down on my knees.

"Lord, won't you please give me a message?" I prayed. "I am not cultured enough and not profound enough theologically for these 'National-socialistic' women." And then came the answer: "Chocolate."

It made no sense to me. Would you call that a message? But suddenly I caught on. I had in my possession a box of chocolate, something that was not on the market anywhere in Germany, to say nothing of in a concentration camp.

The next day I set out for camp full of new courage.

There they were, sitting once more in front of me, resistance and distaste on every somber face.

But I said, "This is my last visit with you, and so I brought you a little treat—some chocolate."

How those faces lighted up! What a luxury a piece of chocolate was to those poor prisoners! All at once we were friends. Some of them even asked me to write my name and address in their Bibles.

When I began to speak, I said, "No one has said anything to me about the chocolate."

"Oh, yes, we did; we thanked you."

"Yes, of course, but no one questioned me about this chocolate. No one asked whether it had been manufactured in Holland or what quantities it contained of cocoa, sugar, milk, or vitamins. You have done exactly what I intended you to do: You have eaten and enjoyed it."

Then I took up my Bible and said, "It is just the same with this Book. If I read about the Bible in a scientifically theological or scholarly way it does not make me happy. But if I read in it that God so loved the world that He gave His only begotten Son, that whosoever (and that means Corrie ten Boom also) believeth in Him should not perish but have everlasting life, then I am really happy. When I read in this Book that there are many mansions in my Father's house, I know that He is also preparing a place for me."

God's Spirit was working. Barriers fell away, and understanding and longing were born in the eyes before me, a hunger to hear more of that love that passes all understanding.

Many months later I was in a large hospital. An emaciated patient seemed to recognize me.

"Don't you remember me?" she asked.

I had to admit, much to my regret, that I couldn't place her.

"Last year I was a prisoner in Darmstadt," she said.

"When you visited the camp, you preached on chocolate. That was the moment of my conversion. Since then I have not read *about* the Bible but *in* it. Now I have to die, but I am not afraid. I, too, have read in His Book that in my Father's house are many mansions. And this I know: Jesus is preparing one also for me."

## 10

*Preaching the Gospel in Word and Deed*

The devil often laughs when we work, but he trembles when we pray.

An invitation came to work in Darmstadt for one week. I was very happy to accept it but asked if it would be possible to enlist the aid of a prayer circle there. Upon my arrival, I found a group of twenty-six people gathered together from the different churches of Darmstadt. I didn't know whether it was their first meeting as a prayer group, but I found them loyal helpers. Every day, a number of the group would meet with me to pray about the work that had been done on the past day and for the work of the next one. Wherever there is such prevailing prayer something is bound to happen, and there was great blessing during that week.

After my departure the group continued to meet in weekly prayer sessions. It strikes me that here is an excellent prayer discipline. The meetings are opened and closed by reading the Word of God. Everyone present prays briefly and clearly. At times they listen in silence to what God may have to say to them, for, most important of all, is the fact that God speaks through His Spirit.

Where men are praying, God will be working.

Returning to Darmstadt a year later, I found the prayer circle still larger. There must have been at least forty in the group.

My first request was for permission to work again in the same concentration camp where I had preached the gospel the year before. But I heard that the camp was empty. Most of the women had been released, and the worst cases transferred to prison.

The refugee problem in Germany, serious as it is today, was tremendous during the first years after the close of war. There were said to be nine million people without adequate shelter. There were the "Umsiedler" from the Russian zone and from other countries behind the iron curtain such as Czechoslovakia, Poland, and Hungary, and then the countless numbers who had been bombed out of their homes.

For a small amount of money we rented the unused camp, and with united efforts made the barracks as habitable as possible. Soon the refugees poured in.

Some of the faithful members of the prayer group took a very active part in the work; I myself traveled on, but promised to return as soon as possible.

Now here I was, back again. The gate was unguarded. The barbed-wire fences were camouflaged by shrubs, or here and there removed entirely.

I walked through the barracks. The work was still in its early stages, and separate rooms had not yet been built. Several families were living together. One of the barracks was locked, and we found that the men who lived there had taken the key away with them that morning. That aroused a bit of suspicion in us; but, even so, we were not prepared for the horrible disorder we found after securing another key to open the door. The beds were unmade, the floor littered with fuel; rubbish was piled high in the corner.

Was it possible that human beings lived here?

"We'll certainly tell these men tonight what we think of them," said the superintendent. But I exclaimed quickly, "Oh, no, please don't scold them. These people have wandered from country to country and from one camp to another, and they have forgotten how to live in a house with love and consideration for it. We must help them. Let's tell them we're going to have a party next Wednesday, and that we expect them to have everything clean and tidy."

The prayer group was enthusiastic about the idea. Everyone had a share in the preparations for the party; and when Wednesday arrived there was a transformation in the main barracks. The tables were covered with white cloths, and there were flowers everywhere, for it was springtime.

Three women and five children had arrived in camp that very day and added to our company. There were refreshments, coffee, cake, white bread, and fruit. We sang roundelays that sounded fine. All of the members of the prayer group were present; and they helped the men, who were at first ill at ease, to feel at home. So there was a pleasant and happy atmosphere, and everyone listened attentively as I spoke to them. I honestly cannot remember ever having attended a more enjoyable party.

During the course of the evening, a thin, shabbily dressed man stood up and clicked against his teacup.

"Friends," he said, "I have been wandering about for nine years. Tonight I feel like a human being for the first time in many years."

We received excellent cooperation in this work from the municipal government and from the Evangelisches Hilfswerk. In their spare time, the men were permitted to build themselves houses in a forest nearby. After some time there were to be two villages, one for five hundred and another for three hundred families. As soon as one family left, other refugees would take its place.

The work grew. A Sunday school was organized for the children, a Bible study group for the women, and every Sunday there were worship services. But the men wanted to spend every spare minute in building their homes and weren't much interested in taking part in the services. Then an original plan was worked out.

There were four neighboring ministers and churches cooperating in conducting the worship services. Each minister and his parishioners, therefore, had a turn once in four weeks. Now, in order to persuade the men to come to church, the ministers and their parishioners decided that the same week in which they conducted the service they would also spend one afternoon building houses.

The gospel in word and deed.

# 11

*Once a Soldier of Hitler*

I am come a light into the world, that whosoever
believeth on me should not abide in darkness.

John 12:46

Germany can be very depressing, not only because of
the ruins of its houses, but even more because of its
many ruined lives.

A young man and I were walking in a pleasant valley
between green hills. The weather was lovely; it was a
spring day, full of promise. Birds were singing, the skies
were blue, and fresh green blossomed on trees and
shrubs. Every year, since the spring season I spent in a
prison cell, I have been doubly thankful for freedom
whenever there is a beautiful spring day.

The face of the young man beside me did not look
happy. I wanted so much to share my joy with him, to
open his eyes to the beauties of nature around him, so I
prayed, "Lord, show me the way; help me to understand
him. Let your love shine through me."

Then he began to speak. He told me about his youth.
At the age of fourteen he had been enrolled in one of
Hitler's schools. It was a fine school, and the boys
had everything their hearts could desire. "When I was

fourteen," he said, "I had my own canoe, at sixteen, my own horse, and at eighteen, my own car. I was nineteen when I became a Storm Trooper and was put in charge of a camp where Storm Troopers were punished for minor offenses. I approved heartily of the rigid discipline maintained there. That was the way to develop a strong and tough generation. I have been reared systematically in hardness and cruelty. There is only one ideal, and that is power. Everything you spoke of in your talks was weak. You spoke of forgiveness. Forgiveness is weakness."

"Can you imagine, Karl Heinz, that forgiveness requires more strength than hatred?"

"Oh, no. Hatred is strong, and forgiveness is weak. Once, when I was seventeen years old, I saw a ship with thousands of prisoners aboard. It was sunk before my eyes, and it did not move me at all. I am well trained."

The loveliness of the spring day was gone. I saw no blossoms, no fresh green buds, only a bird pulling a worm out of the ground. The worm writhed in its beak. It was not the only worm that was being bitten to death.

The young man beside me was not the only German boy who had been poisoned.

Poor world!

I was suddenly dead tired.

"Let us sit down here for a few minutes, Karl Heinz."

A beautiful panorama stretched out before us. We were sitting on the top of a hill and could see far into the distance

The day will come when the righteousness of God shall cover the earth as the waters cover the sea.

In my imagination I could see again the concentration camp. Thousands of prisoners were streaming toward me, and I struggled to go against the tide. Bep was beside me.

What ugly, bitter, and depraved faces we were seeing! I longed to escape the disharmony.

Then Bep said, "I am beginning to love the multitude."

I prayed, "Lord Jesus, come quickly and fulfill your promise to make all things new. Grant that I, and all your followers, may redeem the time, for the days are so evil. Save this young man beside me. Fill me with your love so that it will flow through me and touch him."

When I got back to the place of our conference, Werner said to me, "I saw you leave with Karl Heinz, and we have been holding a prayer meeting for you. Were you able to help him?"

"I don't know, Werner; I prayed continually, 'Lord, make me an open channel for your love.' But look, why don't you have another talk with him?"

"I'll be glad to do that. I understand Karl Heinz perhaps better than you do. I myself was once a soldier of Hitler. Now I am a soldier of Jesus Christ!"

# 12

---

# Holland

> We are the children of a King and have in our possession the key to our Father's storehouse. All its treasures are ours to use at any moment.
>
> *Eva von Thiele Winkler*

I was back in Holland. How wonderful it is to be in one's own country! I love Holland. Nowhere else do you see such colors. Look at that field of grass! It is a different shade of green from the next field, and the one beyond it is still another shade. The moist atmosphere of Holland transforms the countryside into a symphony of tints and shades.

We were sitting on a dike looking far out over the polders and resting after a delightful bicycle trip. There were quite a few of us in the party, and soon some of the group around me began to discuss a sermon we had heard the day before.

"I thought he made things much too simple," said one. "Becoming a child of God isn't that easy."

"But as many as received him, to them gave he power to become the sons of God" (John 1:12).

"Yes, but before you receive Him, you must be elected."

"Certainly, but that is God's business. All you have to

do is obey. If that were not possible it would not have been written 'work out your own salvation with fear and trembling' (Philippians 2:12). And though we do so at times with fear and trembling, the wonderful part of it is that 'it is God which worketh in you both to will and to do.' That means that we are on the victorious side because God is omnipotent.

"He Himself has given His only begotten Son to us that we might have eternal life 'who will have all men to be saved, and to come unto the knowledge of the truth' (1 Timothy 2:4).

"Jesus says, 'Come unto me, *all* ye that labor and are heavy laden, and I will give you rest' (Matthew 11:28, emphasis added).

"There are in the Bible two very important truths on this subject. One is that God rules over this universe and that He is omnipotent; that is God's sovereignty. The other is that we are held accountable; that is human responsibility. Logically, these two truths cannot be harmonized. They are like two ropes hanging from the ceiling not touching each other anywhere. Only if one should look above the ceiling would he see that they are connected and are actually the two ends of one rope.

"We must be careful not to do injustice to either of these truths of Scripture by the analysis of logic. St. Paul states it very clearly in 1 Corinthians 1 and 2. There are two planes or levels. One is that of the "wisdom of the wise," the wisdom of this world. The other is that of the foolishness of God, which is wiser than the wisdom of the wise; this is the love of God that passes all understanding.

"We cannot and must not reduce the foolishness of God, which is the greatest wisdom, to the level of human wisdom. We may do the reverse. If, through the power of

God's Spirit, we lift our logical thinking, which is the wisdom of the wise, to the plane of the foolishness of God, we see that His foolishness is not illogical but superlogical. We then enter the sphere of higher dimensions. God's thoughts are higher than our thoughts.

"We are able to comprehend these things only by faith, the substance of things hoped for, the evidence of things not seen. Faith is the radar that penetrates the clouds of our logical thinking and discerns the love of God that passes all understanding. Theology is the queen of sciences as long as it remains a tool in the hands of the Holy Spirit; but if it is used by man in order to raise barricades behind which he wishes to entrench himself, then it becomes theology in the hands of Satan.

"Now," I continued, "tell me honestly, when the minister spoke to you after the service and asked you, 'Won't you say yes to Jesus now, and surrender your life in obedience to Him,' did you do it? No, you didn't, because that arrow glanced off your theological barrier. You knew very well that to lose your life for Christ's sake would mean to obey Him, and that would involve breaking with your sins, particularly with that one pet sin of yours. You didn't want to do that.

"And right at this point we come back to that glorious divine side of conversion. You realize eventually that you, yourself, cannot break with your sins; but if you turn over the reins of your life into the hands of Jesus Christ, you are at once on the victorious side. For He 'was manifested, that he might destroy the works of the devil' (1 John 3:8).

"Conversion is not, as some may think, a leap into the dark, but a leap into the light, straight into the arms of the Lord Jesus."

# 13

## The Manufacturer of Our Faith

It is not a great faith that we need, but faith in a great God.

I was back again in Germany. It was spring, and people were building everywhere. Ruins were being cleared away. Property owners who did not clear the rubble from their land would forfeit its ownership. Everything was being done as cheaply as possible; no town planning with harmoniously constructed neighborhoods, no lovely homes with bay windows, no beauty either within or without. The people just built wherever they were, in the midst of the ruins, and used old partially burnt or broken bricks. Here and there the ruins themselves were merely patched up, with no effort made to demolish and rebuild. Rooms without exterior walls served as verandas or even as storage space.

In the areas where rebuilding had not yet begun there were shrubs growing in the midst of the ruins, growing where once had been rooms, rooms where people had lived.

Fresh young leaves were coming out on the branches, and their colors were lovely in the spring sunlight. The colors of ruins, too, can be lovely, but their forms are horrible. That is why it was so terrifying to walk in the streets at night.

I had just spoken to a group of young people on the riches we have in Jesus Christ. Germans are very reserved; and when I invited them to remain for a period of discussion after the meeting, it took courage for the seven who accepted to overcome their instinctive reluctance to do so. Once so far, however, the ice was broken.

One of them said, "I am an atheist. You do it with Jesus; I do it without Him, and do at least as well as you." As he told me about his successes in his own strength, I said very little. Debating has never been one of my strong points. I prayed silently for him as I listened, and then said, "If the time should come in your life when you can no longer go on in your own strength, then remember and think about what you heard this evening."

Then another boy began to speak and said, "The Bible is for me an inventory record of all I possess in Him. I followed Hitler with all my heart and soul. But God intervened in my life and took everything away from me. I was a prisoner, and one of my comrades read the Bible with me every day we were in the prison camp. It was then that I came to know Jesus."

Tongues were loosened now, and others began to tell about their difficulties. One said, "I am so unfaithful; I want to believe, but my faith wavers. Now that you have told us all these things, I feel certain again; but what about tomorrow? I don't know whether it will be so then."

I told him that I was a watchmaker by trade, and that in our shop we received sometimes new watches that did not keep good time. These I did not repair myself, but sent back to the manufacturer. When he had repaired them, they ran accurately. And that is also what I do with my faith. Jesus is the "author and finisher of our faith." If there is something wrong with my faith I send it back to the heavenly manufacturer. When He has repaired it, it functions perfectly.

It is fortunate that Hebrews 12:2 does not read "Let us look unto our own faith."

If I should do that, I would perhaps say, "My faith is great." That would be pride, and the victory would be the devil's. Spiritual pride is very destructive.

Or if I should say, "Oh, my faith doesn't amount to anything; it doesn't do anything for me." That is defeatism; and it, too, is a victory of the devil.

Hudson Taylor once said, "We do not need a great faith, but faith in a great God."

Let us therefore look more and more to Jesus and not upon our own faith. Let us look not upon the storms around us, but keep our eyes fixed upon Him. Then we shall be able to walk upon the waves of the turbulent sea of life. Faith is such a firm foundation that the safest place for a Christian to walk is the water that Peter trod as he went to meet Jesus.

Our conversation just naturally turned into prayer, and even the "atheist" folded his hands and closed his eyes.

# 14

*Intercessory Prayer*

Jesus Christ is able to untangle all the snarls in your soul, to banish all your complexes, and to transform even your fixed habit patterns, no matter how deeply they are etched in your subconscious.

My technique of working has developed only gradually through experience. I prefer now to speak to the same people eight times, reserving forenoons for personal consultations, and having a period for discussion after every evening meeting.

In Germany it is not easy to get people to talk. They have had training in keeping silence. It was very dangerous for anyone to express an opinion during the Hitler regime. Now again there is fear, for to show one's colors these days may involve one in serious difficulties in the future.

So when I announced, "This meeting has now come to a close, but all those who would like to remain for a while to converse about these things are cordially invited to do so," it was merely the signal for emptying the church lecture room within two minutes.

That was definitely not the right method, and I prayed for wisdom.

The next evening I clothed my invitation differently, saying, "The meeting has now come to an end, and we shall have a period of discussion. Will all of those who must or wish to leave, kindly do so at this time?"

Now it took courage for people to stand up and leave, and so they remained seated. When it had required courage to remain, they all left.

We had a very lively discussion. Questions came from all directions. And I prayed, "Lord, let me be only a channel for Thy Spirit; I am not equal to this."

Then I experienced a miracle. Even before a question had been completely stated, I already knew the answer.

I knew, of course, that such group discussions did not provide the real heart-to-heart contacts, so the morning hours for personal conferences were very important. It is when we are alone with people that we come close to them. And it was during these hours, more than anywhere else, that I could hear the cry of a wounded Germany.


This morning a woman came to my room. Her face was pale and embittered; about her head she had wrapped a black scarf. The Germans can sometimes display their misery in such a dramatic way.

It seemed to me that darkness entered the room with her, and I prayed, "Lord, cover me with Thy blood."

She began to speak in a complaining tone, and her sermon, like all good sermons, had three points. The subject of point one was how very bad people are in general, the Christians in particular, and the preachers worst of all! Point two was how very good she herself was. She talked about her virtues and the good deeds she had done. Then followed point three as conclusion. How is it possible that people dare to say that there is a God when such a good woman as herself should have so sad a life, such poor health, and so tiny a room in which to spend her days?

When she had finished she looked at me as if to say, "And now of course you will quote the Scriptures to me."

"I have a word for you," I said.

"Oh, have you?" I could see her thinking, "Here it comes"; but I said mischievously: "Edel sei der Mensch, hilfreich und gut." (Let man be noble, helpful, and good.) It was a quotation from Goethe, who is again greatly admired and faithfully read in a large part of Germany today.

The woman's reply was unexpected, "But I cannot fill my empty heart with that."

I looked at her in surprise.

But I had more to say to her: "Jesus has said, 'Come unto Me, all ye that labor and are heavy laden, and I will give you rest'" (Matthew 11:28). Then I gave her one rich promise after another from God's Word, and a miracle took place before my eyes. The woman drank in every word thirstily, as though parched for the water of life.

Never before had I witnessed such a sudden change in attitude. When she left the room, I knew she was a changed person, not yet a converted one, but a person who had opened her heart to the truth and was eager to know more of it.

Immediately after she left, a gentleman entered the room and said, "I've already waited an hour to see you."

"I'm sorry; I didn't know you were here. But it would have been impossible to cut short our conversation."

"It is really quite all right," he replied, "I made good use of the time. I could hear snatches of your conversation from the next room and began to pray for you, for I realized you were having a hard time."

"When did you begin to pray?"

"Half an hour ago."

When the man began to pray, the miracle happened: The woman opened her heart to the gospel.

How little we realize the great importance of intercessory prayer! If at this moment you pray for someone, even though he is on the other side of the globe, the Lord Jesus will touch him.

"I did not come to see you about myself," continued the man. "There is in this town a woman who is in great need, and I came to ask if you would perhaps try to contact her. She has refused to see any of us, though we have prayed much for her. You may succeed where we have failed."

"I would be very happy to try. What is her name and address?" He mentioned her name. It was the name of the woman who had just left my room, and I exclaimed, "But that is the very woman who was here a few minutes ago! You will be able to reach her now, for she is longing to know more about the gospel. You have prayed for her, and now you may thank God."

When we intercede for a person with God, we are participating in God's economy of salvation. This means nothing less than that we have opened our hearts to God's Spirit, who prays within us. Could that be the reason why it also operates within ourselves in such a saving, releasing way?


I once traveled by car through the mountains of California from Los Angeles to San Francisco. It is one of my weak points that I am afraid of driving through mountains with Americans. They usually drive at such great speed. Along one side of the road was a deep chasm, and, moreover, there were many dangerous curves. I knew from experience what to do when the demon of fear entered my heart. He had called on me many a time during my imprisonment in Germany, and I would then begin to sing. Singing always helps. Try it yourself some time; fear and anxiety will vanish when you sing.

So I sang one hymn after another, until my host, the driver, said teasingly, "Are you afraid?"

"Yes," I said, "that is why I am singing."

But this time it was all to no avail. Every time we approached a curve, I would think, "If another car is coming towards us from beyond that curve, we shall certainly crash into each other!" And, thoroughly frightened, I would stop singing.

No, singing did not help me now. Then I tried to dispel my fear by prayer, and I prayed. But my prayer became a refrain: "Lord, bring us safely to San Francisco. Do not let us crash down into this abyss. Please grant that there will be no car approaching us from around that curve ahead."

I kept on praying to dispel my fear, until suddenly, and I do not know how the idea came to me, I began to pray for others. I prayed for everyone who came into my thoughts: people with whom I had traveled, those who had been in prison with me, my school friends of years ago. I do not know how long I continued in prayer, but this I do know, my fear was gone. Interceding for others had released myself.

Some time ago in San Diego, I met a man who told a story of the power of intercessory prayer. He had been a heavy drinker and was finally taken to a psychopathic hospital. Here he was placed in a room with three other patients, who did nothing but scream. When night came he was in despair. He prayed but could not fall asleep while the screams continued. Then suddenly he began to pray for the three patients, and just as suddenly the screams ceased.

"Not only that," continued the man, "it seemed as if something broke in me. When I prayed for others, my own tension was released, and I was free. The next day I had to undergo a psychiatric examination. At its conclusion the doctor said, 'There is nothing wrong with you; you are normal.' I knew that night that I had become a free man."

Intercession often adds to its many other blessings the healing of one's own tension.

# 15

## Refugees in Distress

O'er the ruin within, around us
Shines the star of Bethlehem.
In our sin and need it found us
And it led us to our King.
O'er the ruin within, around us
Heaven's light is shining still;
God in mercy has unbound us
From the night of Satan's will.

Hundreds of refugees were living in a big factory. The machinery had been taken away, but every corner of the building was in use as living quarters for the persecuted people who had found rest there.

Rest?

I was in a hall where about two hundred people were living together. It was like an enormous house without partitions. Around a table, children were doing their school work. Behind them were beds, and behind the beds was still another "room." Girls were getting ready to sleep. Farther on there lay men who had just returned from work. Dead tired, they had stretched out on the mattresses.

Most of the people had already lived there for three

years. Though everyone was rather quiet at that moment, there was a murmur of many voices and the stir of a great number of people. There was no privacy, no room for anyone to call his own. It reminded me of a big waiting room, but it was not that at all. People were not waiting here in order to leave; this was where they lived.

One could easily see the difference in degree of prosperity between the various family groups. Here in one place were beds with thick eiderdown quilts and elegant bedspreads, and a lamp with a lovely shade standing on a colorful Persian table cover. Right next to it there were a couple of mattresses on the floor with soiled blankets and without sheets. A woman was cutting black bread on a dirty wooden table.

The superintendent who showed me around the place said, "Now why don't you give these people a message? If I ask for silence all of them will be able to hear you."

But I shrank back, "Oh, no, please; not today," I begged. "I cannot speak here now. I would like to come back later on to live with them. Perhaps then I will dare approach them, but I can't just step in from the outside, to say a word, and then go back to my own peaceful guest room."

After two months I returned. But I came at a bad time. There was a strong feeling of opposition toward all Christians. A minister had done a very stupid thing. He had visited the factory and then written a newspaper article describing the situation there in very roseate terms. After reading his article one would almost be tempted to ask for permission to live in the factory, even though one had a small home of one's own. The occupants of the factory were justifiably indignant, not only with the minister in question, but with all Christians in general. As a result an evangelist who had worked there among the children had been refused admission. Moreover, a paper had been posted near the entrance stating that no one who called himself a Christian would be permitted to enter the place.

I did not allow myself to be intimidated by all this, but went to the police and inquired about the possibility of having myself registered as a refugee.

"But you are not a refugee," the police officer said.

I explained the situation to him, and he was amused. I was registered, and shortly afterward I walked into the factory right past the prohibitory paper.

The situation inside had improved. Ropes had been stretched from one wall to the other, and over the ropes were hung blankets or newspapers that had been sewn together and fastened to the lines by means of clothespins. In this way, everyone now had at least something that resembled a room of his own. During the day I was to stay with a married couple; and sleeping arrangements were made on the other side of the "street," where a bed had been placed for me in a little "room" occupied by two women. I was to do my own cooking and had already bought some eggs and tomatoes. When I asked my hostess to lend me a pan, she called out, "Who will lend a frying pan to the newcomer?"

A frying pan appeared from under the blanket partition, and I went downstairs to the basement, which had been fitted up as a kitchen. The heat there was unbearable. Big stoves were going full blast, and around them women were doing their cooking, as many as forty of them around one stove.

It was interesting to see how the menus of the various nationalities differed from one another. The Germans as a rule cook starchy foods, many potatoes, sometimes with macaroni as a substitute for vegetables, and followed by pancakes for dessert. There were women from Latvia, Poland, and Czechoslovakia, and all of them had different menus. My little meal of eggs and tomatoes, though rich in vitamins, was not regarded with appreciation, and certainly no one would have been willing to exchange food with me.

I left the overheated kitchen as soon as possible and, in the company of my hostess, ate my first home-cooked dinner as a "refugee." We sat on a little bench and ate from a box that served as a table. It cannot be denied that there was a certain atmosphere of snugness between the paper partitions, but the sounds and odors from all the other "apartments" penetrated unhindered into our "room."

Then I started what was actually to be my work here. From one "room" to another I went "calling." I talked little but listened much and gazed into the depths of suffering and joyless existence. Most of the people were the discouraged ones, who no longer had enough energy to work themselves up from this level of existence. Dispirited and embittered at the same time, they told me about their flight from bombings and their wanderings from one camp to another until they had here found their "home."

Some of the people had adapted themselves amazingly well to their new surroundings. But such surroundings! Unemployed men and boys were playing cards in a bored sort of way. Women were trying to tidy up their "houses." There was a nasty fishy smell in the building.

Some women were doing their cooking, and odors of food mingled with those of cigarettes, cheap perfumes, jute, and other unpleasant scents. The sun burned down on the glazed roof. I lived on the attic floor, and its small windows were closed.

A little girl walked directly across our "room" toward her own "home." She simply pushed the newspaper and blanket partitions aside.

Somewhere in the building a woman was screaming. She had come to get her daughter, who had been held here during the night. Whether it had been against her will or not, I was unable to find out. Things happened here just as they do in many quarters of the big cities where the poor, the unemployed, and the desperate live together. But the difference here was the sounds were unrestrained by partitions.

Everyone stopped talking and listened to hear the end of the row. After the woman had gone, life resumed its course and sounds: the whining of a mouth organ, the complaining cry of a sick child, the snapping of an over-strung mother, the thumping of romping boys, and the uninterrupted buzzing of more than two hundred voices.

Was there any rest to be found in this place? I visited the people and tried to talk to them. I listened to their stories of misery and flight. "Would things ever become better in this world?" they asked me. I could speak only about the future of Jesus Christ, of His second coming, and of the new earth wherein righteousness shall dwell. For this world I see so little hope left. There is only hope for this world in the light of 1 Peter 1:6: "Though now for a season, if need be, ye are in heaviness through manifold temptations." It is the light of Jesus Christ that continues to shine in the most profound darkness, the light that is victorious on behalf of those who know and love Him. To them, all things work together for good.

Was there still hope for this part of the world, where nine million refugees were crowded into the houses that still remained standing in this bombed-out land of ruins, for a country where the remaining factories were being blown up, where unemployment was increasing day by day, and where the means of subsistence had simply vanished?

I thanked God for my experiences in the concentration camp. Now I could tell these people about my experience of the reality of Jesus Christ in the hell of Ravensbrück. The fact that I also had suffered aroused their interest, and I was entitled to speak, because I could understand them.

In the evening my host came home. He borrowed a stool from the neighbors, and after supper two elderly men entered with their stools and, crowded together, they smoked their pipes in the little "newspaper room." I was tired to death when I lifted the "blanket door" of the neighbors and entered their room to get ready to sleep. It was a good bed they had made up for me. As I stretched out on it, everything that I had experienced that day passed before my mind's eye like a film.

At Ravensbrück I had had good training in casting all my care and burden upon Him of whom it is said, "[Cast] all your care upon him; for he careth for you" (1 Peter 5:7). My suitcase of cares was full to the brim, and when I emptied it before the Lord I prayed, "Lord, here they are; help me now to leave them with Thee and continue my way unburdened."

There was noise all around me. What an unrest! Then suddenly out of the confusion of sounds around me, a conversation struck my ear. On the other side of the paper partition, two men were planning how they would deal with a Christian who might be bold enough to enter the building. I didn't hear the end of their discussion, because I was already asleep before they stopped talking. The last thought that came to mind before I fell asleep was "underneath me are His eternal arms."

# 16

## Chairs in the Camp

I will instruct thee and teach thee in the way which
thou shalt go.

*Psalm 32:8*

While living in the factory I received an invitation
from the InterVarsity Christian Fellowship to work
for ten months among its student groups in American col-
leges and universities.

Life in the factory had tired me out. It was the last
one of the ten months that I intended to spend in
Germany. The work there had been very gratifying, but at
the same time very fatiguing. As I read the letter, a great
longing arose in me to visit the United States. The
Americans are less complex than the Germans. Of
course, they have not come through such terrifying times.

I didn't know what to do. I wanted very much to go to
the States, but I knew that if it was God's will for me to
continue my work in Germany, He would also renew my
strength. I only wanted to know where He was calling me.

So now I asked for a miracle, a sign. Was that per-
missible? Certainly: Gideon did.

"Lord, if it is Thy will that I should go to America,
then grant me free passage. That will be a sign to me. I

know that Thou art willing to grant me money for the trip, but I cannot help thinking how many chairs I could buy for the camp at Darmstadt with that much money."

I knew now how uncomfortable it was to have no chairs. When my friends and I fitted out the camp at Darmstadt we did not have enough money to buy chairs. Beds, clothing, food, all of the barest necessities, we were able to procure, but we had no money for chairs.

When I talked these things over with my friends they said that it indicated that I should not go to America. Why not? God is a God of miracles. He would be able to grant me free passage.

I went to the office of a shipping company in Amsterdam. "I want to go to America," I said, "and would like to work for my passage as a stewardess." I could see some humor in the situation, for, after all, I was no longer very young, and it was questionable whether I would be able to do such work.

"Do you know that stewardesses are allowed to spend only one week in America? They have to return on the same boat."

"Oh, no. I intend to stay in the United States for ten or eleven months. But will you allow me to tell you something about my life story?" I asked. "During the war—"

"Wait, you don't have to say another word. I know all about it. Here is your book *A Prisoner and Yet . . .*; I know your entire story. Isn't it wonderful that God actually called you to work in Germany?"

"Yes, it certainly is, but how do you know about that?"

"I have always been interested in your activities, and it will not be my fault if you don't succeed in obtaining free passage."

He arranged everything for me. I was to travel on a freighter, presumably as a stewardess.

The occupants of my camp at Darmstadt got their chairs, and the most wonderful thing about it as far as I was concerned was the assurance that it was God's will and His guidance that I should go to America.

# 17

———— ∞∞∞ ————

# Hollywood

But as many as received him, to them gave he power
to become the sons of God, even to them that believe
on hs name.

*John 1:12*

I had been invited to attend the meeting of a prayer
group of film stars in Hollywood; and I was excited,
waiting to see what would happen.

It was indeed a group of fine looking people. They
received me cordially but very informally, and at first I felt
a bit out of my element.

After one of them had read the Scriptures to us, they
all knelt down, and I was moved as I observed a gladness
and thankfulness in their prayers such as I had seldom
witnessed before. When I spoke to them I found them
open-minded, and afterward some of them told of their
experiences. "I was so happy when I got to know the Lord
Jesus," one of them said. "That week I had to play a dramatic part in which I was supposed to cry. I simply could
not cry. I was too happy."

Some of the stars told of their "suffering shame for His
sake." Like many other Christians in the United States,
they abstain from drinking and smoking. Therefore it soon

became known that they were Christians, and people asked them, "Don't you smoke? Are you a member of a Sunday school?" Then when they professed their faith courageously, they sometimes had to face derision and contempt from their colleagues.

A young and pretty girl named Colleen Townsend said to me, "I'll remain in the film world until God makes it clear to me that I must leave it. We are the only people who can approach our colleagues, and we want to make use of our opportunities as long as possible."

Three weeks later I read in the paper that she had resigned from her very lucrative job and had become a Bible school student.

The second time I came into contact with this group was at their gospel meeting, which was held every two weeks for their non-Christian colleagues. The meeting was held in the home of Jane Russell.

Her house is really extraordinary. It is situated on top of a mountain, and the last part of the road to it is so steep that it is accessible only by car. One wall of the living room is made entirely of glass, and from this vantage point there is a magnificent view of Hollywood. The structure of the room and the furniture are most unusual and have a decided charm.

A young minister spoke that evening, and brought his message of sin and salvation with great earnestness but interspersed with real humor. He showed that the greatest of all sins is unbelief and the will to resist Jesus Christ. Not only the demand of conversion, but also the great joy of being a child of God, he proclaimed in such a way that it really inspired his entire audience. With no hesitation whatever, he described the future of those who are lost, an eternity without Jesus Christ.

Sing-Sing and Hollywood. The extreme east and the extreme west of the United States. Nowhere else have I witnessed such an interest in and open-mindedness for the glad tidings.

Later in Holland, when delivering a lecture on America, I told my audience about this experience in Hollywood. During the discussion someone asked me, "How is it possible to be a film star and a Christian at the same time?"

I prayed for wisdom to answer that question, and then said, "To combine the frivolous life of a film star with Christianity is practically impossible. But equally impossible are the combinations of pride and Christianity, self-sufficiency and Christianity, irreconcilability and Christianity, backbiting and Christianity."

It reminds me of the story of Jesus and the adulterous woman. "He that is without sin among you, let him first cast a stone at her" (John 8:7). And Jesus Christ is very serious in His command to the film stars and to all decent and indecent sinners: "Go, and sin no more" (John 8:11).

How wonderful it is that He came into this world to save sinners! On Calvary we see the awful sinfulness of sin, but we also behold Him, "The Son of God [who] was manifested, that he might destroy the works of the devil" (1 John 3:8).

"For we are his workmanship, created in Christ Jesus unto good works, which God hath before ordained that we should walk in them" (Ephesians 2:10).

When we are hidden with Christ in God, then we are on the victorious side.

# 18

---

# *In London*

God is willing to enter into the heart, as light is willing to flood a room that is opened to its brightness.

*Amy Carmichael*

In London I was asked to call on a woman in a mental institution. The one who had fallen a victim to hatred. She had always lived in Palestine. Her husband had been kind to the Jews, and then it was the Jews who had dropped a bomb on their home. When she regained consciousness and saw that her husband was dead, she opened her heart to hatred. Now she was a complete wreck. She spent the whole day reading the newspapers in order to find news about the Jews. If something terrible happened to them she was happy.

Poor woman!

As she entered the room she looked suspiciously at me. I prayed for wisdom and love.

"I know exactly what you're to tell me. I must pray," she began the conversation in a defiant manner. "But I cannot pray."

I made no reply, and she continued, "I know exactly what you are going to say next; I must banish the hatred from my heart, because only then can I pray again."

"Who has told you that?"

"The chaplain."

"No doubt the chaplain is still a very young man, and he does not know how powerful the devil of hatred is. You and I know. Once I was with my sister in a concentration camp. When they treated me cruelly I could stand it, but when I saw that they intended to beat my sister, because she was too weak to shovel sand, then hatred tried to enter my heart. And then I experienced a miracle. Jesus had planted His love in my heart, and there was no room left for hatred. The only thing you can do is to open your heart to that love. That love is a reality. If it is dark in a room, while the sun is shining outside, do I have to sweep the darkness out? Of course not. I merely have to draw the curtains aside, and as soon as the sunlight floods the room the darkness vanishes."

We both knelt down, and I prayed, "Lord, here we are, weak, much weaker than the devil of hatred. But Thou art stronger than the devil of hatred, and now we open our hearts to Thee, and we give thanks to Thee that Thou art willing to enter into our hearts, as the sun is willing to flood a room that is opened to its brightness."

A week later the woman was discharged from the mental institution. Her heart was full of the love of God.

# 19

⬸⬸⬸

## May

For this purpose the Son of God was manifested, that
He might destroy the works of the devil.

*1 John 3:8*

In the middle of the woods was a little summer house.
May and I were taking a walk along the cliffs near
Lynton on the west coast of England. We had heard the
day before an impressive lecture on the demand of
unconditional surrender to God.

We rested in the summer house for a little, and May
used the time to scoff at the lecture. Not only the content
but the structure too was given a thorough going over.
May just tore the lecture to shreds. I looked at her and
couldn't help smiling.

"What is the reason for all these objections? Is it perhaps because you do not want to do what is demanded of
you? Have you ever surrendered completely? In John 3 we
read the story of a man who came to Jesus. He was told
that 'except a man be born again, he cannot see the kingdom of God, neither can he enter into it.' Has that 'being
born of God's Spirit' already taken place in your life?

"God's Spirit is here, He wants to dwell in you, but
you have to make the choice. Does that seem so difficult?

Not so long ago it was a choice between Jesus and a world of progressive and expanding civilization. Now it is a choice between Jesus and a world of rapid decline.

"You can make it seem very complicated, but isn't it much like a proposal of marriage? What kind of answer does a young man expect when he asks a girl to marry him? Certainly either yes or no; there is no other possibility. So it is when we choose between Jesus and the world. Jesus says, 'come unto me,' but your answer is no, because there is something behind your criticism, isn't there?"

"Just the same, I would like to surrender to Jesus," she said. "My whole heart is longing for peace with God. Actually I know the way, but when I am on the point of saying yes a barrier seems to arise and keep me from surrendering."

"Listen, May. Think back over the events of your life and tell me if you have ever been in touch with spiritism. Have you ever been to a fortune-teller? Do you know that when you do such a thing you fall under the spell of it, through which the way to God becomes barred for you? Yes, even the way to conversion. Such a spell may ensnare you even if you have just allowed yourself to be treated by a mesmerist. Very often such people are also on the wrong side, and that may be a great danger."

May laughed in a mocking way. "As a matter of fact, I did allow myself to be persuaded to go to a fortune-teller years ago," she said, "but I did not believe in it; I did it only for fun. Afterward we had a good laugh about it. I had completely forgotten about it, but now that you ask me, I remember it very well. But surely, there's no harm done; I did not believe a bit of it."

"May, suppose you were a solider during a war and

you had to reconnoiter a certain terrain. By mistake you fell into the enemy's hands by entering his territory. Do you think that it would help if you then said, 'Oh, excuse me, please, it was not my intention to come here; I just came here by mistake?' Once you are on their terrain, you are at their mercy. Though you did not know it, a demon has taken possession of your heart, and your life has fallen under his spell. When you want to be converted he comes in between. You don't understand the significance of it, and that's why it is so dangerous. St. Paul says in Ephesians 6:12, 'For we wrestle not against flesh and blood, but against principalities, against powers.'"

The look of amusement had left May's face, and fear was there instead.

"I'm not telling you these things to make you afraid, May. If I had no more to say than this it would have been better to keep silent, but the first step toward victory is to know the enemy's position. And the wonderful thing about it is that Jesus is the victor. He is far stronger than all the powers of hell. What you have to do is to close the door exactly there where you opened it. I mean this; think of one of the Scripture passages that speaks of forgiveness."

May thought for a moment, and then said, "Colossians 1:14, 'In [His dear son] we have redemption through his blood, even the forgiveness of sins.'"

"That is right. Now ask the Lord Jesus to go back with you to that very moment when you committed that sin. Confess your sin, ask forgiveness, and give thanks for it, because the text, which you quoted, is true. Then the door is closed and you are free. Then you are no longer at the demon's mercy.

"I myself once had the opportunity of showing the way of salvation to a fortune-teller. It was in Germany.

The whole day long she was busy 'closing doors.' Then she came back to me and said, 'I feel happier, but I know that there are sins that I have forgotten. I am not completely free yet.'"

"'Just tell the Lord Jesus about it as you did to me and give thanks for forgiveness,'" I replied.

"Two days later she returned and said, 'This morning I awoke singing. I am completely free.' She was full of praise and thanksgiving to the Lord.

"Will you do it too, May? I know for a certainty that you'll be victorious. I'll leave you to yourself now. Fight it out the rest of the way without me."

I left her alone and walked back to the conference grounds. The surf was pounding against the cliffs. A storm was coming up, and it was a tremendous sight. Near the shore a steep rock rose abruptly out of the sea. It was as if two powers fought against each other, but the rock stood unmoved amidst the waves.

On the last night of the conference, the leader asked if any would tell what they had learned and experienced these weeks. May stood up and said, "I have learned and experienced here that Jesus is victor."

# 20

## Switzerland

It is foolish to underestimate the power of Satan, but it is fatal to overestimate it.

I had the privilege of speaking for three successive evenings in a little church built against the slope of a mountain in Switzerland. I was a guest in the beautiful manse and enjoyed the conversation with the minister, the splendid view from my bedroom window, and the pure mountain air.

On the last evening I spoke on the reality of the promises of God. Often we do not understand these promises. They seem too lofty and beyond our comprehension, and so we lay them aside without really giving them serious thought. But that is not God's intention. He is back of every promise with His love and His omnipotence, and He was in great earnest when He made them. Therefore I believe that we are sinning when we ignore them or perhaps evade them by theologizing them away.

My train was not leaving until the following evening, and so the next afternoon found me standing outside the manse, gazing at the beautiful panorama spread out before me. Far in the distance were snow-clad mountaintops, and in front of them rose the green slopes of the foothills. The sky was bright blue, birds were singing exuberantly, and I myself was humming a hymn of praise to my Creator: "Never can faith expect too much."

Callers arrived to see me; a mother and her fifteen-year-old daughter. The child was a pitiful sight, for she cringed in fear at the slightest sound and buried her face in her mother's arm. The mother's face was full of sorrow as she looked at me pleadingly.

"You spoke last night on the reality of the promises of God," she said. "Do you believe that yourself?"

"Yes I do," I answered instantly. "God's promises are a greater reality than our problems."

"Then for Christ's sake cast out this demon," she said vehemently.

I shrank back as though she had struck me. Anything, but not that! That was a terrain on which I did not want to venture. Other people might be able to do so, but not I.

I prayed silently and asked, "Lord, you know that I cannot and will not do this."

The Lord answered me clearly and unmistakably. "But you must do it, because there is even more truth in what you just said to the woman than you yourself realize. My promises are true."

The mother and I read Mark 16, and then we prayed together and asked Jesus Christ to cover us with His blood and give safe protection in every struggle against, or attack of, the devil.

I asked the child, "Do you know the Lord Jesus?"

"Yes," she said, "but I wish He would make me happy. I want to be happy."

Then I spoke to the demon, in the name of the Lord Jesus, who has gained the victory on the cross and who has cleansed us with His blood. In His name I commanded the demon to come out of the girl and to go back to hell, where he belonged. I forbade him to enter anyone else or to possess the child again.

The poor girl left that manse as much possessed as when she came, and I was profoundly unhappy. How weak I was in faith, and how lacking in power! Was it only theory that I had been preaching, theory that failed when I tried to put it into practice?

I knocked on the door of the minister's study. He received me kindly. "I need your help," I said. "My faith was too small, and now you will have to do it," and I told him about my experience.

He looked up at me, startled, and said, "Oh, that is a sphere I refuse to enter."

"But who must do it then? You are the shepherd of this flock, and you have God's promises. Please, read Mark 16:17."

He took his Bible and read, "And these signs shall follow them that believe; In My name shall they cast out devils." And verse 20: "And they went forth, and preached every where, the Lord working with them, and confirming the word with signs following."

The minister buried his face in his hands. His reading changed to prayer, and I heard him whisper, "Forgive me, Lord, that I have neglected my duty."

Great joy entered my heart. This was the reason I had to experience the failure of my own attempt. This shepherd had to learn something, and God used me as His instrument.

When I left in the evening there was no darkness, but only gratitude in my heart. There was still much that I didn't understand, but everything was all right.

Jesus is Victor.

Two days later I received a letter from the manse: "Corrie, something wonderful has happened. When the mother and her daughter crossed the threshold of their home the demon went out of the child. This morning both of them came to me full of praise and thanksgiving to Him who was really serious about the promises He made to us in the Scripture. My husband wants to know if you will come again, and this time stay longer than three days."

But I knew that this would not be necessary. Jesus is Victor, and He uses everyone who is willing to obey Him.

Whate'er the love of God would do
Is never by His power denied.

# 21

---

## *Unpaid Debts*

We rob the work of Jesus Christ of its efficacy, and
we stand powerless before the adversary, because we
doubt the integrity of the Word of God.

A young minister was taking me to the station.
I learn so much in conversation with people. I
wish that everyone who works at spreading the gospel
could travel as I do, for it is a daily source of knowledge
to meet so many people. One does not accept everything
he hears, of course, any more than he accepts all that he
reads in books. But as in eating fish one picks out the
meat and lays aside the bones, so also in conversation;
and one learns much in the process.

We had had a blessed meeting. God's Spirit had been
at work, and now I asked the minister whether he had any
scruples about the message. There are not many people
who are willing to be frank enough to criticize the message of another, but it is just through such honest criticism that one learns most.

"Now that you ask me," he replied, "I will tell you. I
thought your message was good, but I didn't like your
terminology. You spoke on the blood of Jesus. That is a
term I should prefer to leave to the sects."

Though we had met only recently, I still felt sufficiently free to correct this young man and said, "You are
in worse company than I am. The devil has a great aversion for that very term; in fact, he hates it even more than
you do. I am in better company, that of the apostles Paul,
John, and Peter. And, do you know, as I looked around in
your church I saw many who were under the curse of evil
powers?"

"Not merely under a curse!" he exclaimed. "Many in
my congregation are possessed by demons. It is terrible,
and I am powerless against it."

"Isn't it possible that your lack of power is a direct
result of your suppressing this important doctrine of the
Bible's message? We read in Revelation 12:11, 'And they
overcame him [the devil] by the blood of the Lamb.' Let
us take joyously the sword of the Spirit, which is the
Word of God, and let us not weaken our position by using
only that which is beautiful and attractive to us in the
Bible or what we can accept on the basis of reason."

We continued our talk for a long time; and when the
train was on the point of leaving, he said laughingly,
"Perhaps there is some truth in the statement that the
sects are often the unpaid debts of the church."

# 22

## Bermuda

He that abideth in Me, and I in him, the same
bringeth forth much fruit: for without Me ye can do
nothing.

*John 15:5*

There was a woman tourist in Bermuda who used her
vacation time not only for rest and recreation but also
for spreading the gospel. It was a time of great blessing for
her, and after returning to her home in Jenkintown, she
was faithful in intercession for the people living in that
beautiful island. Together with her prayer group, she
prayed that many of them would accept the gospel.

Is there any better preparation for revival than that of
a group of people praying with one accord? Can there be
work more important than intercessory prayer?

It was during a visit to this friend that she asked me if
I could arrange to go to Bermuda for a week. As far as
time was concerned, it was possible to add it to my schedule. But I did not have money for the plane trip. So I
asked the Lord for guidance. When it became clear that
He wanted me to go, I wrote immediately to Bermuda
saying that I would come; the matter of money I
entrusted to the Lord. Within two or three days, checks

arrived from different people, people who knew nothing of the proposed trip. And there was just enough money for a return ticket.

The plane was approaching land.

The gray water beneath us turned to blue, as if a huge ink well had been emptied into the sea. I saw white houses and a lot of green, and as we came down, gorgeously colored flowers everywhere.

What a beautiful bit of land! The setting sun added brilliance to the many colors.

Customs officers, clad in white uniforms, searched our luggage. One of them looked at my papers and said, "Miss ten Boom, I'll take care of you as quickly as possible, because our prayer group is waiting for you. Then we'll go right over." This was a promising welcome: from the airport directly to a prayer meeting! It looked as though this would be a week full of action.

And it was! At the prayer group that evening there was evidence of great interest, a genuine thankfulness for the message, and a desire to know more about the gospel. It was the beginning of a week of blessing such as I had never experienced before.

My schedule was more than filled. There were at least twenty speaking engagements, and there was scarcely any time for preparation between the successive addresses. I could not, nor would I, object, for I had asked them to give me as many opportunities as possible in order to make the most of my visit. I ran short of sleep because the post-meeting discussions often lasted far into the evening. Sometimes, however, I could sleep a few minutes between gatherings.

Whenever I spoke, I would ask all who were willing and able to pray during the meeting that God would make me an open channel for His Word, and that His Spirit would work in the hearts of the people. I felt myself upheld also by the prayers of my friends in the United States, who were in sympathy with me and who expected much of this work.

The very first morning a young man came to interview me for the Press. We found it possible to pray together, and he became an important and loyal helper in the work. He was present at all twenty meetings, and each day there was an excellent and accurate report of my messages. The result was that my talks became known to many who had not been to any of the meetings, and that in turn created possibilities for other less formal contacts.

The work was quite varied and took me from a nursery school class of the cutest children to a dignified Rotary Club meeting, from the island prisons to its churches. And in between were many conversations, sometimes on the street, or in stores or offices.

On the narrow winding roads my "manager" drove me from one place to another. Traffic keeps to the left, of course, since Bermuda is English territory, and cars are not allowed to travel faster than twenty miles an hour. But on this island there is time enough for everything.

As the car pulled up at our destination, a black man walked over and said, "I never knew that there were real children of God among the white people, but since our prayer meeting I know better." And then he added, "God gave you a good training in your work among the feeble-minded in Holland. Now you speak so simply that all of us can understand you." I myself had often thanked God for that part of my experience, but it surprised me that this man had observed the importance of it so quickly.

My talk to the Rotary Club was broadcast over the

radio, and in it I paid the Press a compliment, saying, "I have often read the greatest nonsense about myself in the newspapers. One time, for example, I read that I had released thirty-five thousand prisoners in Germany. Here in Bermuda, however, the Press is excellent. The main points of my talks are very correctly reported. I have been in many places, but nowhere else have the news reports been as good as here."

Next day a headline on the front page of the daily paper announced in big letters: "Corrie ten Boom says Bermuda has the best reporters in the world." But the nice part of it was that they now put forth even more effort than before to give me good publicity.

So everything worked together for good. God's Spirit was busy in the hearts of people. The messages that made the greatest impression were these: that the problem of sin has been solved on the cross; that the devils and demons are conquered spirits; and that our struggle is a struggle of faith, through which we come to see the victory of Christ.

It was a great privilege to preach these glad tidings also in the prisons. Something happened there among the prisoners. The first time I spoke, one man stood up and said, "Come back again. We understand you and love to hear the things you tell. Please come again. We are not as bad as some people think." I was permitted to speak several times, and the prisoners were also allowed to hear my four radio addresses. So we learned to know one another quickly. The last time I visited them one prisoner arose and asked, "May we sing 'Just as I am, O Lamb of God, I come'?"

"Yes," I replied, "but only those who will truly come to the Savior either for the first time or for recommitment."

As long as I live I shall not forget the faces of those men as they sang, deeply moved, earnestly, yet joyously, "O Lamb of God, I come." Before the second stanza, I said, "Now only those who wish to possess the fullness of God's Spirit." And then again, "Now sing it as a testimony to your neighbor."

Afterward, a rough-looking man with an unshaven face came up and presented me with a small cedar box. He had worked on it for months. Another prisoner pressed my hand and said, "I am a child of God."

The warden told me that the prisoners talked all day about what they had heard.

After this visit, there was a final meeting in the church. My first talk had been the Sunday before to a handful of people in a basement room. Now the church was filled with both white and black people, something that is said to be unusual in Bermuda. The sisters and brothers could not restrain their joy. Their "Hallelujah's" and "Praise the Lord's" resounded through the church. In conclusion, I announced the same hymn the prisoners had sung, "Just as I am, O Lamb of God, I come." I told the audience what had happened in the prison, and added, "They who do not sing this straight from their hearts will be preceded by the prisoners in the kingdom of God." I knew that the prisoners were listening, because this final meeting was also being broadcast. And what a meeting it was!

Afterward a white woman came up to me and said, "Do you suppose this is the beginning of the revival for which we have been praying so long?"

Bermuda, an island of great natural beauty, with colors everywhere! Deep-blue water, trees with brilliantly colored blossoms, fields full of lilies, white houses.

Bermuda, an island of friendly people. Some of them had taken me to a store and said, "Now you must buy something for yourself. No, this money must be spent on something for you. We won't allow you to use it for the work in Europe." Then they debated what would be beautiful enough for me.

Suddenly there flashed into my mind a picture from the past. As a despised prisoner in Scheveningen, I had not been permitted the luxury of walking on the corridor runner. It was too good for me, though it was nothing but a coarse coco-mat; I had to walk alongside of it. Gray, colorless prison! Was God favoring me especially now in giving me the enjoyment of the gay and brilliant colors of this paradise and majestic island far out in mid-ocean, and the love of these warmhearted islanders?

What has been the happiest experience of this blessed week? Just this: the privilege of dispensing the great riches of God's Word to people who do not tire of listening to it, to people who are hungering for the gospel and never become satiated with it; to be allowed to speak from early morning until late in the evening about the promises of God, which are greater and have greater reality than our problems; to speak of the love that He requires of us but which He Himself supplies to us. And I prayed, "O Lord, do let me have more such experiences as this one. I want to work obediently only where you call me; but do call me to places where people are as hungry for the gospel as in Bermuda, and where I may dispense as lavishly of Thy great riches. It is so wonderful to be able to share abundantly with others. O Lord, who am I, to have been so privileged? Thank, you, Father, for these eight days, the most wonderful days of all my four years of traveling."

———

Then came Cleveland. I was staying with dear friends of mine, but there was not much opportunity for me to speak in their church: one evening meeting, poorly attended; and then I was allowed to speak for fifteen minutes to the children in the Sunday school. And I was discontented. Only a Sunday school! No, compared with this, Bermuda knew how to appreciate Corrie ten Boom.

What a success for the devil! Just imagine! The Lord Jesus stayed up half the night for one man, Nicodemus, and He considered it important enough to explain the most beautiful part of the gospel to this one man. See John 3! But I didn't think it worthwhile to preach the Word to a group of children, children, with their whole lives still before them, children whose roots are not yet so deeply planted in the earth as those of adults. Young saplings are so much easier to bend than old tree trunks. But pride had found its way into my heart. And right there things began to go awry—and though the beginning of a path be ever so slightly awry, its end will be far afield.

Chicago was next on my schedule, but no word had come to confirm my appointments there. I therefore decided, without waiting guidance, that it was just as well to go a day later. Moreover, there were some unexpected opportunities to speak in Cleveland, so I sent a telegram to Chicago to inform them that I would arrive two days later.

A friend was waiting at the station in Chicago when I arrived.

"Why didn't you come at the appointed time?" was his first question. "You have missed two important engagements."

Startled, and also a bit chagrined, I answered, "Why didn't you write and confirm our arrangements?"

"We couldn't. You failed to send us your Cleveland address."

How ashamed I was!

Everything in Chicago went further and further awry. I missed connections and seemed to do the wrong thing at every turn. I was glad when the time came for me to leave for Holland, Michigan.

The first evening with my friends there we talked and talked.

"How was Bermuda?"

"Oh, wonderful! What a place! Such lovely people! And how hungry they are for the Word of God! It is so beautiful there, whole fields of lilies, flowering trees, deep-blue sea!"

"And how was Cleveland?"

"Oh, nothing out of the ordinary." And I began quickly to speak again about Bermuda.

"And Chicago?"

"An awful place to be in summer. Stiflingly hot, both night and day. No, give me Bermuda."

That evening I had a long talk with the Lord. I had often said to people, "If there is a shadow somewhere in your past of which you do not like to be reminded, stop where you are and take it to God in prayer. Ask Him to retrace your steps with you to that dark spot, 'For the blood of Jesus Christ cleanseth from all sin,' and His presence changes the darkness into light." Now it was my turn to put the precept into practice, and I prayed, "Lord, go back with me to Chicago and Cleveland. What was wrong there?"

The answer was very clear: "Cleveland and Chicago, that was Corrie ten Boom without Me. Bermuda, that was Corrie with Me."

Now I could see it. What a privilege it is to see the reality of things! Yes, the reality of our own sins, and unworthiness, and inadequacy—but in the light of the victory of Christ.

"Without Me ye can do nothing," said the Lord. "I can do all things through Christ which strengtheneth me," said Paul (Philippians 4:13).

The branch of the vine, without Him, bears no fruit at all, but with Him, much fruit, even a hundredfold.

# 23

## Finances

His is the gold and silver of the whole earth, the cattle on a thousand hills.

On my early trips to the United States I used to speak at times on the need in the Netherlands and Germany, and on the work that we do there, and then ask that people support our work financially.

In general, Americans are very liberal. The many parcels they have sent to the poverty-stricken countries of Europe during the post-war years bear witness to their liberality; and those parcels, in the great majority of cases, did not come from the wealthy. I have often been present when American housewives were preparing such parcels. Every time they went shopping they bought something for Europe, and these purchases were set aside in a specially reserved place. I wonder if they used their "tithe" for this? Many Christians place a tenth of their income aside for the work of God, and they remain faithful in this even in times of scarcity.

Preparing these parcels is not an easy job! There are many forms to fill out; and the weights and measures of the parcels have to meet certain requirements. Only then is the parcel taken to the post office.

"Thank goodness, that package is off! And fortunately it was not too heavy!" the tired housewife exclaims. Then they continue—how often I've heard them: "But I'm so glad to be able to do something for the people of Europe who are living under such trying conditions."

It has really been quite a job. As a rule American housewives have no easy life. They are often employed outside the home also in order to earn extra money, and their evenings are frequently taken up with endless church and social gatherings. Many people in Europe think that all Americans are wealthy, but that is not true. Generally they have to work as hard as anywhere else in the world to keep their heads above water.

People in America do not seem to think it strange when a speaker from Europe asks for a collection to be taken for the work there, but I myself sometimes felt that there was something wrong about it.

I had been speaking on the need in the Netherlands and in Germany, and after the meeting a dignified and well-dressed woman came up to give me a sum of money for the work in these countries.

"It was so very interesting to hear about your work," she said.

"What did you think about the other things of which I spoke? Did you find them important also?" I asked. "Of course it is a very good thing to give money for evangelistic work, but today I spoke also on conversion. God does not want only a little of our money, He wants our hearts. Because of His great love He wants to possess you completely. The Lord Jesus wants you to come to Him with all your cares, with all your sins, with all your unrest concerning the past, with all your fears about the future. He says: 'I will give you rest.' Let Him hold the reins of your life. Then you will understand that His yoke is easy and His burden light, and then His joy will fill your heart; for it is His intention 'that [His] joy might remain in you, and that your joy might be full'" (John 15:11).

While I was speaking there came a haughty look into her eyes. Very coolly, she took her leave with no response whatsoever to my comments.

When I got back to my room I looked sadly at the money she had given me. Was there perhaps something wrong in speaking of one's own work and at the same time on the need of conversion? When I prayed about it the answer was very clear: "From now on you must never again ask for money."

Great joy entered my heart, and I prayed: "Heavenly Father, Thou knowest that I need more money than ever before, not only for traveling expenses and for the house in Holland, but also for the camp in Germany. But from now on the little evangelization work of the 'ten Boom Foundation' will be carried out on the same basis as the great mission work of Hudson Taylor. I know that Thou wilt never forsake us."

That day I received two letters. One was from a woman in Switzerland. "Corrie, God told me that from now on you must never ask for money again," she wrote. The other letter was from my sister in Holland. She wrote: "When I prayed for your work this morning God made it very clear to me that you should not ask anybody for financial support. He will provide everything."

I thought of the night in the concentration camp when my sister Bep and I had talked about our plans. "Corrie, we should never waste our energy in collecting money. God is willing to supply our every need."

And now this repeated charge, in Switzerland to my

friend, in Holland to my sister, and here in the United States to me. God takes his prohibition of asking for money seriously, just as He means it seriously that He will care for and protect us. He is willing and able to supply our every need according to His own riches; we may trust in that promise one hundred percent.

# 24

⸗⸗

# The Second Coming

Then we which are alive and remain shall be caught
up together with them in the clouds, to meet the
Lord in the air: and so shall we ever be with the Lord.

*1 Thessalonians 4:17*

We were sitting in a park under the shadow of a
large tree. A conference was being held in the
stately house behind us, but today the weather was so
beautiful that we could have our meeting out in the park.
The view of the lake, with a dense forest in the distance,
was lovely.

Our gathering at this time was not an official one.

I had mentioned a couple of times in my lectures the
second coming of the Lord Jesus, and several people had
expressed a desire to know more about this subject. So I
offered to tell them what I knew about the subject some-
time between our scheduled sessions.

I began by giving them an illustration: "A telephone
operator was called each day by the same person and
asked for the time. After some months of this she asked
the inquirer for the reason of his daily call. 'At twelve
sharp I have to give a whistle signal,' the man said.

Startled, the girl answered, 'And I always set my watch by that very whistle signal.'"

That is the world today. There is no foundation, no certainty, no safe objective standard.

The Bible, however, is our Standard time.

"Give me a place outside the earth on which to rest my lever and I will move the world," Archimedes said.

We possess this "Archimedes' fulcrum" in the Word of God.

The great blessing of our time is that the world is aware of the fact that it is bankrupt. The widespread middle-class contentment, which gave the world its false sense of security up to forty years ago, has vanished. The whistle signal has deviated too much from true time, and as a result people have lost confidence in it. These are the days in which the trumpet of every Christian must sound no uncertain note.

The world complains that there is no longer a future. But we find in the Bible that one out of every twenty-five texts speaks of the assured future of the kingdom of God at the coming of His Son. There is no one who fears His coming so much as the devil; and it has been a victory of the devil that the greatest consolation that the Bible grants us has been changed into a subject of theological controversy.

Jesus Himself, Paul, Peter, and John all state in unmistakable language that there will be a point in time at which Jesus will return. This momentous event will be so glorious to them who belong to Him that it is written, "Wherefore comfort one another with these words." Then they will be with the Lord forever. To those who do not love Him there will be judgment and tribulation. It is very clearly written, "But exhort one another daily."

There will be signs of the times, of which we must be observant. To those who do not belong to Him, Jesus will come "as a thief in the night," but the children of God "are not in darkness, that that day should overtake you as a thief" (1 Thessalonians 5:2, 4).

One of the most outstanding signs of the times is the return of the Jews to the land of Israel. Frederick the Great of Prussia once said, "If one wants to know the time on the clock of world history, let him observe the Jews."

Our confession of faith speaks of the second coming of Christ only as the judgment of the living and the dead. To those who are in Christ this judgment will be the glorious moment in which they will be manifested as the redeemed.

To the world the second coming of Christ will mean the end of Satan's dominion over the world, the end of the rule of the prince of this world. For Jesus is coming to take possession of His own inheritance. It will be an invasion by the Owner Himself who has promised: "Behold, I make all things new" (Revelation 21:5). Then "the earth shall be filled with the knowledge of the glory of the Lord, as the waters cover the sea" (Habakkuk 2:14). Therefore, those who love His appearing, pray with John, "Even so, come, Lord Jesus" (Revelation 22:20).

"But I don't understand anything of all that I am hearing," said a young woman. The other listeners, too, admitted that this was unfamiliar territory to them. Yet this conference was not being held for unchurched laymen. All of these people were attending the conference because they desired, more or less, to discuss and to be trained in the methods of proclaiming the gospel in their own surroundings. To these convinced Christians, the second coming of Christ was totally unfamiliar ground.

"When the Son of man cometh, shall he find faith on the earth?" (Luke 18:8).

# 25

## Two Little Girls

The Bible is not a frozen bank account.

A mother whom I was visiting brought two little girls about ten years of age to me. One of the girls was her own daughter, the other her foster child.

"Will you tell them how to become children of God?" she asked. "Both of them attend Sunday school; they know something of the Bible, but over and over again they ask me, 'How can I become a child of God?' I don't know how to explain that to them."

We were in a village high in the mountains of Switzerland. The small house was on the edge of the village, and there was a beautiful view of the Alps.

I prayed to the Lord for wisdom. We have the promise in James 1:5, "If any of you lack wisdom, let him ask of God, that giveth to all men liberally." God's promises are true. I have an idea that God is pleased when we confront Him with His promises; He then knows that we have faith.

I sat down with the two girls on a bench in front of the house. "Now look," I said. "Just suppose that I wanted to adopt one of you as my child. That wouldn't be easy. First of all I'd have to fill out many papers. It would take a long time before everything was in order. But even when all the papers were found to be correct, I still wouldn't say to you, 'Everything is arranged, now you are my child.' No, I would wait until I knew that you really loved me a little, and then I would ask you some day, 'Would you like to become my child?' Then if you answered, 'Yes, please, for I love you,' I would say, 'Then everything is settled. Here are the papers. They were ready for a long time, but I was waiting until you, yourself, told me that you loved me and wanted to be my child.'

"Just so, the Lord Jesus arranged everything on the cross a long time ago. All that was necessary to make you a child of God was finished many centuries ago on Calvary when He died for your sins. And now He asks you—and I may do it in His name—'Do you want to become a child of God?'

"If you say, 'Yes, please, Lord, for I love You,' then He'll say, 'Everything is settled now; I have been waiting a long time for that answer; now you are My child.' Do you want to give the answer now to the Lord Jesus?"

Both of them spontaneously knelt down, and in their amusing Swiss-German language they said yes to the Lord; and the angels in heaven above rejoiced.

Their faces were radiant with happiness, and they were more beautiful than the mountains on the horizon. The sun had set, but the "Alpen-glow" changed the world into a bit of heaven. For some time the three of us continued to talk about the world of riches that the two little girls had now entered.

Children of God.


Once more I saw mountains before me in the sunset glow. But now I was on the other side of the world. I was attending a meeting of students in the State of Washington on the West Coast of the United States. We sat around a campfire and were having a wiener roast. We speared the frankfurters on pointed sticks and roasted them in the fire.

The topic of our conversation was conversion. A boy asked, "How do you bring yourself to the point of conversion? Just what do you do to bring it about? You talk as if it were such an easy thing to do in order to become a child of God."

Was it the mountains in the distance that suddenly reminded me of the two little girls in Switzerland? I told the students about my experience, but one of them said, "I said yes to the Lord many years ago; what do you suppose is the reason that I've retrogressed so much since then? I sometimes doubt that I meant it seriously at the time."

A tall medical student answered him: "Once there was a boy who fell out of bed. His mother asked him how he happened to do that, and he answered, 'Mommy, it happened because I fell asleep too close to the place where I climbed in.' That is also what happens to many Christians. When they are converted they think that they have reached the goal. When one is converted and says yes to Jesus, it does not mean the end of a new experience, but the beginning of it. It is as if one had entered a gate, the gate of conversion. To enter into the kingdom of heaven through the gate of conversion means to enter into a world of riches. All the promises in the Bible become your property. But you have to learn to find your way around in that world of riches. You have to find out what it means 'For all the promises of God in Him are yea, and in him Amen' (2 Corinthians 1:20). You have to find out how rich you are. If you think conversion means that you have arrived at the end of the pathway in your life, you will fall out, for then you fell asleep too close to the place where you climbed in."

Then I added, "At the moment of one's conversion he is registered in heaven as one who has earned all the rights and privileges that make one a multi-millionaire in a spiritual sense. Ephesians 1:3: He 'who hath blessed us with all spiritual blessings in heavenly places in Christ.'

"The Bible is a checkbook. When you said yes to Jesus Christ, many promises were deposited to your credit at that very moment, and they were signed by the Lord Jesus Himself. But now you have to cash your checks in order to profit by them. When you come upon such a promise and say, 'Thank you, Lord, I accept this,' then you have cashed a check, and that very day you'll be richer than you were the day before."

"Let's sing," a student suggested. The mountains re-echoed the hymn, "Every Day with Jesus Is Better Than the Day Before." One student remarked, "That's really true, at least if you cash no less than one check a day."

## 26

---

# The Children of Light
# May Not Walk in Darkness

Firemen who straighten pictures in a burning house.

I was speaking at an American university on the subject of evangelism.

"If I straighten the pictures on the walls of your home, I am committing no sin, am I? But suppose that your house were afire, and I still went calmly about straightening pictures. What would you say? Would you think me merely stupid or very wicked? Why, you'd say I was not only stupid but wicked as well.

"The world today is on fire. What are you doing to extinguish the fire? Are you sitting in your study formulating theological concepts? Are you in training for a tennis tournament? These things are both good in themselves; but what are you doing to put out the fire? Your communist brothers are busy forming cells. What are you doing?

"A communist has written, 'The only people who can help the world in its present condition are the Christians; but they do not realize it.'

"Don't you understand? Has Jesus not said, 'You are the salt of the earth, the light of the world'?"

The children of light!

The next morning I was walking in the garden of the beautiful campus with a pretty coed. "Tell me," I said, "What are you doing to bring the gospel to your fellow students?"

Her lovely face colored as she said, "I feel very guilty this morning. I see myself suddenly as very much like the fireman who goes around straightening pictures while the house burns. I am a very self-conscious person. I have given my heart to Jesus, and I know that I am a child of God. But there is still a part of my shy retiring self living within an enclosure deep inside of me, and I become furious with anyone who approaches that enclosure. I have always felt that I had a right to live my own life. Recently I gave my testimony at our club meeting, and they told me that my language and style and voice were quite good. So I know that I could speak in public. But if I should do so, people will see behind the enclosure, and that I will not have."

"Jeannie, it is only when we are crucified with Christ that we can enter into the joy of His resurrection. That sounds bad, but it is a loss that turns out to be a great gain. 'Whosoever shall lose his life for Christ's sake, shall save it.' Then you will find that His yoke is easy and His burden light. The time is short. To be lost for eternity is a dreadful thing, and to be used in saving others is such a wonderful experience."

People should see that we are ministers of Christ, to whom the stewardship of the mysteries of God has been entrusted. In the final analysis, the one requirement of such stewards is that they be "found faithful" (1 Corinthians 4:1–2).

In many places in the United States, prayer meetings

are being held regularly for the specific purpose of praying for a revival. The privilege of speaking at these meetings with these people who are not merely grateful that
they themselves are saved, but who also are full of love
and compassion for a world lost in sin, always constitutes
a high point in my life. I feel at home with people who see
where the only solution really lies.

But there is another prerequisite for revival, besides
that of prayer. For those who are seriously in earnest
about this matter, there must also be a very personal and
complete readiness to throw themselves wholeheartedly
into the cause of the gospel. Everything must be placed
on the altar.

I once heard a sermon by the Reverend Oswald Smith
at a conference in Switzerland. The following made a
deep impression on me.

He held four books in his hands and asked, "Is everything on the altar? Have you lost your life for Christ's
sake, your money, your time, your family, your home?"

He placed the four books on the table. "This is my
money; this, my time; this, my family; this, my home. Yes,
my money, all of it, except a small savings account that I
have laid aside for my vacation.

"So, not all of my money." And he took one book from
the table.

"My home, yes, except that I cannot take the children
of my sister who is ill. They are so unruly that I just can't
have them as guests in my home.

"So, not my home." And he removed the second book
from the table.

"My time? Yes, it all belongs to the Lord. But my two
weeks' vacation? I have a right to that, and have already
reserved a room at the hotel.

"So, not my time." A third book disappeared.

"My family, yes, but I have not allowed my daughter to become what she so eagerly wishes to be, a missionary. We have a large family, and she must stay at home to help her mother.

"So, not my family." He picked up the fourth book.

The altar was empty.

I left the conference room and went out to walk alone, and I searched my heart. Was everything in my life on the altar? I was deeply touched. I understood very well what Oswald Smith meant. It was not a question of God's permitting His children to have their vacations. "Shall He not with Him also freely give us all things?"

"But seek ye first the kingdom of God, and His righteousness; and all these things shall be added unto you."

But in this losing for Christ's sake there may be no exceptions on our part. "Everything, Lord, except this one thing" will not do.

Can we rejoice in the resurrection life without having been crucified with Christ?

How much compromise there is!

I often wonder how it is possible that so many Christians live like beggars when we are royal children, the very children of God. We appropriate one or two of His promises, but most of them we negate, or ignore, or—reject.

If indeed we have been "blessed . . . with all spiritual blessings in heavenly places in Christ" (Ephesians 1:3), why then do we still so often sigh? Are we really saved? Or is the devil right when he accuses us day and night? Is it true that we have been made "the righteousness of God in him"? (2 Corinthians 5:21).

Nietzsche has said, "Maybe I would have believed in

a Redeemer if the Christians had looked more redeemed." Is it not written in Romans 5:5, "The love of God is shed abroad in our hearts by the Holy Ghost which is given unto us." Why, then, do people not see that love in our eyes? We so often live like carnal Christians.

Are we to be saved as by fire, and our works burned? (1 Corinthians 3:15).

This I do know, that we are living far below the level of what we actually are in Christ. How can this be? Is it perhaps that we do not really want to lose our lives for Christ's sake? If we want to save our lives we shall lose them.

May we then pray for a revival among others?

What about our churches in this respect? Does my church rejoice to learn that a revival has started in another church that is perhaps much more fundamental or more modernistic than ours? Will they be glad to hear that twenty people have been converted in that particular sect from whom they differ so much on the subject of chiliasm?

"That they all may be one; as thou, Father, art in me, and I in Thee, that they also may be one in us: that the world may believe that thou hast sent me" (John 17:21).

No?

How, then, can my church pray for a revival?

And what about my readiness to forgive the sins of others? Are the sins of my fellow Christians in the depths of the sea? Is the reputation of all absent persons safe in my keeping? Or are their sins so firmly anchored ashore that if you should ask me anything about them I can tell you immediately all about their irritating or unlovely characteristics?

If this be true of me, may I then pray for a revival?

If I have so little understanding of the reality of God's promises that my problems seem greater than the victory of Christ, may I work toward a revival, even to the extent of praying for it?

Revive the world, O Lord, beginning with me!


Later on, I spoke to another group of students on the subject of revival and mentioned among other things these high demands for those who wish to join in preparing for revival by praying for it.

"That means that I may not pray for a revival," said Lucy.

What? Was that to be the result? Had I made a mistake in establishing such lofty requirements? Should I be a little less positive about these things next time? Perhaps a bit of compromise might be more pedagogical?

That afternoon, Lucy and John took me with them in their car for a lovely trip through the mountains. It was a beautiful day. We picnicked in one of the state parks deep in the forest and later saw a magnificent sunset. The sky seemed to be suffused with the silhouettes of buildings and towers, which made it look like a fairyland of beautiful colors; gold, green, rose, and blue.

"Do you think heaven will look like that?" asked Lucy.

"When you stand at the gates of heaven you will have a bird's-eye view of your life," I replied. "I have often had to face death. It seems that then you see reality, you see the things in their proper perspective: the great things great, and the small things small."

"I think I shall see my sins as very large then," said Lucy.

"How do they look to you now?"

"Also very large. When you spoke about the lofty requirements we must fulfill before we may pray for a revival, I could see that I hadn't come nearly far enough to be equal to it."

"And do you just accept that situation?" asked John.

"Well, yes, I guess that's the way I am. I am a child of God, but certainly not a bit better than other Christians. After all, we are only human beings."

"From which direction do you suppose that remark came, from the Spirit of God or from the devil?" I said.

"I think, very likely, from the devil."

"And do you believe what he says? Don't you know that he is a liar from the beginning, and that he can do nothing but lie and deceive? If I always lied and boasted would you still listen to me? Of course you wouldn't. Why, then, do you listen to the devil?

"Do not forget that he is a conquered enemy. Jesus was sent to destroy the works of the devil. We do not have to take the responsibility for one single sin. 'If the Son therefore shall make you free, ye shall be free indeed' (John 8:36).

"Just think about what you said this morning: 'Then I may not pray for a revival.' Here is our world, so utterly bankrupt and unhappy that even the most indifferent person can see that we are headed for destruction. Not only are millions of people living without Christ, but they are facing an eternity without Him. We have seen in the course of history that revivals are used by God as a means of saving thousands of people for eternity. What you can do to help in this work is to pray for it with others. But you cannot do this as long as you hold on to your egotism, your selfishness, your pride, or whatever is your besetting sin.

"'All right then,' you say; and you cling tightly to your ego and your sin, thinking that it is quite all right, and that life is even very pleasant that way. You don't see that you are bound, hand and foot, that you are losing your life by trying to save it.

"You do want to enjoy the resurrection life with Christ, but you refuse to be crucified with Him daily and to die unto self. The result is not only that you lead a poverty-stricken spiritual life, with little in it of the victory of Christ, but that this bleeding, perishing world is minus one more intercessor. Do awaken and see the reality of this truth. Give up your life for Christ's sake, and you will save it. Sanctification is not a burden but a blessed release."

By now the sun had set, and darkness was closing in around us, although the sky was still suffused with gold. But before we started the homeward journey all three of us made a new commitment of ourselves to Him who prayed:

"As thou hast sent me into the world, even so have I also sent them into the world. And for their sakes I sanctify myself, that they also might be sanctified through the truth" (John 17:18–19).

# 27

## Everlasting Life

Nothing shall be able to separate me from the ocean of God's love, in Christ Jesus.

As far astern as one could go on the deck of a freighter, I found a quiet spot where I could be delightfully alone.

I leaned on the rail and gazed at the silver wake left by our boat on the surface of the sea. Dolphins were leaping out of the water. Seven seagulls were circling around the ship. They would follow us faithfully until land was again within sight.

I mused.

What a tiny cockleshell our vessel is on the immensity of the sea!

What a minute, insignificant, and temporal creature I am! Between my birth and my death I am permitted to live on this earth for some time and after that . . . eternity.

Where am I exactly?

Here I am aboard a tiny ship, and deep, deep under me is the sea, full of the mysterious life of marine animals. Above me is the infinite sky, out of which a tempest might come to wreck this little vessel. Around me is the endless sea, in which so many people have drowned.

Where, exactly, am I?

I live in a world where demons rule, where wars are waged, where hopelessness, cruelty, and fear predominate, where millions of people are starving in China, where cities are turned into ruins in many parts of Europe, where atom bombs are surpassed in destructive power by hydrogen bombs.

Exactly where am I?

I am in a world which God so loved, "that he gave his only begotten Son, that whosoever believeth in him should not perish, but have everlasting life" (John 3:16).

I am on an earth where soon He shall come, even He who has promised, "Behold, I make all things new" (Revelation 21:5).

One day the earth, this beautiful earth, "shall be filled with the knowledge of the glory of the LORD, as the waters cover the sea" (Habakkuk 2:14).

Where am I exactly?

Already, at this moment, I am in Him.

And underneath me are His eternal arms.